MUSHROOM

By the Same Author

The Triumph of the Fungi:
A Rotten History

Carpet Monsters and Killer Spores:
A Natural History of Toxic Mold

Mr. Bloomfield's Orchard:
The Mysterious World of Mushrooms, Molds, and Mycologists

MUSHROOM

Nicholas P. Money

OXFORD
UNIVERSITY PRESS

OXFORD
UNIVERSITY PRESS

Oxford University Press, Inc., publishes works that further
Oxford University's objective of excellence
in research, scholarship, and education.

Oxford   New York

Auckland   Cape Town   Dar es Salaam   Hong Kong   Karachi
Kuala Lumpur   Madrid   Melbourne   Mexico City   Nairobi
New Delhi   Shanghai   Taipei   Toronto

With offices in

Argentina   Austria   Brazil   Chile   Czech Republic   France   Greece
Guatemala   Hungary   Italy   Japan Poland   Portugal   Singapore
South Korea   Switzerland   Thailand   Turkey   Ukraine   Vietnam

Published by Oxford University Press, Inc.
198 Madison Avenue, New York, New York 10016
www.oup.com

Oxford is a registered trademark of Oxford University Press

Library of Congress Cataloging-in-Publication Data
Money, Nicholas P.
Mushroom / Nicholas P. Money.
p. cm.
Includes bibliographical references and index.
ISBN 978–0–19–973256–2 (hardcover : alk. paper)
1. Mushrooms.   I. Title.
QK617.M644 2011
579.6—dc22
2011009269

3 5 7 9 8 6 4 2

Printed in the United States of America
on acid-free paper

For Diana

Nature alone is antique, and the oldest art a mushroom.
> —Thomas Carlyle (1795–1881, Scottish essayist)

Some day the delights of a mushroom hunt along lush pastures and rich woodlands will take the rank of the gentlest craft among those of hunting, and may perchance find its own Izaak Walton.
> —Charles McIlvaine, *One Thousand American Fungi* (1900)

a sun struck stinkhorn
sticky with flies
thrusts up under
the skirt of an oak

—Tom Pickard, *Stinkhorn,* from *Hole in the Wall:*
New & Selected Poems (Chicago: Flood Editions, 2002)

CONTENTS

CONTENTS

PREFACE

As you will have gathered from the title, this is a book about mushrooms. Mushrooms are fungal sex organs and the most wondrous inventions of the last billion years of evolutionary history on earth. If you have missed out on these elemental facts of life, there's no reason for self-flagellation—the next 200 or so pages will soon bring you up to speed.

Mushrooms that appear overnight in a meadow or on a suburban lawn are a marvelous sight. Their growth process is pneumatic, with the inflation of millions of preformed cells from a button extending the stem, pushing earth aside, and unfolding a cap above the dewy grass. Once exposed, a mushroom's gills—arrayed on the underside of its cap—shed an astonishing 30,000 spores per second, delivering billions of microscopic particles into the air in a single day, cells that may be capable of spawning the largest organisms on the planet. Mushroom colonies, gargantuan or lilliputian, burrow through soil and rotting wood. They feed and spread wherever plants live and die. Roll over a rotten log or brush aside some damp leaves, and you'll find white bundles of fungal filaments; squeeze a handful of forest topsoil and inhale its mushroomy fragrance—the rich perfume attending death and decay. The colonies of many mushrooms hook into the roots of forest trees and engage in mutually supportive symbioses; others are pathogens that decorate their food sources with hardened hooves and fleshy shelves. Among the staggering diversity of mushroom-forming species, we find strange apparitions, including gigantic puffballs, phallic eruptions with revolting aromas, and tiny "bird's nests" whose spore-filled eggs are splashed out by raindrops.

Yet, it is the poisonous effects of a handful of fungal metabolites, and the powerful hallucinogenic qualities of others, that account for the central place of mushrooms in mythology and their commonest associations in Western culture. In the twenty-first century, the latest generation of mushroom worshipers promotes the medicinal benefits of fungal extracts, and a global industry has evolved to market these elixirs for soothing every human ill. Mushrooms are also celebrated in modern cookery, and our appetite for wild and cultivated fruit bodies has enjoyed fantastic growth in the last decade. While the appearance of mushrooms in children's stories and the countercultural infatuation with "shrooms" has made everyone more aware of the fungi, this familiarity may also have handicapped their scientific study. Indeed, despite their primal role in supporting planetary health, fungi remain the least studied and most poorly understood kingdom of life.

Getting people to grasp the importance of other familiar groups of organisms can pose similar challenges for scientists. Consider insects. Everyone who has taken a biology class knows that there are millions of insect species and that they perform all manner of life-sustaining tasks, but the only arthropod of immediate concern is the cockroach waggling its antennae at you from the kitchen floor. Facts about all kinds of things can be explained to us—mind-boggling, fascinating, consciousness-shattering conclusions about life and the universe—yet we spend much more time thinking about how much to spend on a bottle of wine on the way home from work, the eternity of nothingness after death, and other daily trivia. But if you have the shopping questions covered, fed the cat, and dealt with your e-mails, I hope you enjoy reading this book half as much as I have enjoyed researching and writing it.

The eight chapters that follow are interwoven and include some cross referencing, but they may be read as independent essays. They explain what mushrooms are (Chapter 1), how they work (Chapter 2), and what their underlying colonies do (Chapter 3); address the harvesting and conservation of wild mushrooms and the cultivation of domesticated species (Chapters 4 and 5); explore the science of poisonous and hallucinatory fungi (Chapters 6 and 7); and uncover deceptive claims about medicinal mushrooms (Chapter 8).

Nicholas P. Money
Oxford, Ohio
January 2011

ACKNOWLEDGMENTS

This book would not have been possible without access to the incomparable collection of mycological books and journals housed in the Lloyd Library and Museum in Cincinnati. Many of the illustrations in the book were scanned from originals in the Lloyd's collection. My sincere thanks to Maggie Heran, director of the Lloyd, archivist Anna Heran, and other staff members for their help throughout this project. Mike Vincent (Miami University) and Mike Klabunde (College of Mount St. Joseph) provided indispensable assistance by translating Latin and Greek passages from original sources. Sushma Shrestha (Miami University) provided invaluable help by researching the medicinal mushroom literature that is discussed in the last chapter. Permission to reproduce Tom Pickard's poem *Stinkhorn* was provided generously by Flood Editions, Chicago. I also thank my editor, Tisse Takagi, for her unstinting support of my work, and my previous editor, Peter Prescott, who helped develop the concept for this book. My wife and scientific collaborator, Diana Davis, read every word of the manuscript, and so please refer any objections to her as the responsible party. I disown any of the book's errors and faults.

MUSHROOM

Chapter 1

Angels on the Lawn

HOW MUSHROOMS DEVELOP

A grown-up neighbor in the English village of my childhood told stories about angels that sat upon our shoulders and fairies that lived in her snapdragons. Like the other kids, I searched her flowers for a glimpse of the sprites, but agnosticism imbibed from my parents quickly overruled this innocent play. Yet, there *was* magic in my neighbor's garden, and I had seen real angels on her lawn: little stalked bells that poked from the dew-drenched grass on autumn mornings, evanescent beauties whose delicately balanced caps quivered to the touch. By afternoon they were gone, shriveled into the greenery. Does any living thing seem more supernatural to a child than a mushroom? Their prevalence in fairy-tale illustrations and fantasy movies suggests not. A reliable piece of scenery behind unicorns, providing forest shelters for elves, mushrooms are often the only things in these stories drawn from reality. Like no other species, the strangeness of fungi survives the loss of innocence about the limits of nature. They trump the supernatural, their magic intensifying as we learn more about them.

This celebration of the fungal fruit body begins, like every mushroom, in the air. On breezy days, the wind is full of invisible biology. Fungal spores—thousands or millions of them in a cubic meter of our life-sustaining gas—accompany pollen from flowers, crop plants, and cone-bearing trees, as well as countless bacteria and viruses. These spores come from innumerable species that blanket the leaves and stems of plants, fungi that feed on animal dung and rot corpses, and the thousands of species of basidiomycete fungi that form mushrooms. We are bathed in a soup of these procreative morsels and inhale the biosphere with every breath. If that doesn't make you reach for nasal spray, consider that each mushroom that elbows itself from the ground sheds hundreds of millions, even trillions, of microscopic spores. As a source of airborne particulates, the mushroom is a masterpiece of natural engineering.

Mushroom spores can start forming a colony when they make landfall at that rarest of sites: moist soil that isn't crowded with other fungi and predatory bugs. This highlights a crucial point in understanding mushroom biology and in assessing the value of mushrooms in the restoration of damaged ecosystems—issues that will be addressed in later chapters. Vast numbers of spores are dispersed because most of them alight on hostile soil. Consider the blood-foot mushroom, a common species in North America. Also known as *Mycena haematopus*, this little orange mushroom weeps a bloody fluid when its stem, or "stipe," is severed (Plate 1). Able to grow on well-rotted, pulpy wood, it is abundant in rain-drenched forests with plenty of fallen timber. Thousands of spores sweep from the bottom of this mushroom's cap every second of its brief life. In perfectly still air, the spores descend at a speed of about one millimeter per second, which means that free fall from the bottom of the blood-foot gills is over in less than one minute. Yet, the slightest breeze can keep the particles aloft for hours. Experiments show that most spores fall quite close to the parent fruit body, many directly beneath the cap, where they are evident as a dusty drape; a few drift much farther through the trees and escape the canopy.[1] With all the wood in a forest, it would seem likely that a large number of spores settle on their preferred food sources. The actual number of successful landings is impossible to estimate with any accuracy, but even among these winners, most perish. Exposed patches of wood aren't as inviting as they might seem. The spore may be eaten by a springtail, slug, or amoeba before it germinates; it may dry up in the withering ray of a sunbeam or get washed away by a raindrop. Its survival is not favored. The woody landing place of a spore may lack the nutrients that the fungus requires: perhaps its relatives have already digested the necessary foodstuffs of its finicky blood-foot diet. Starvation is a reliable reaper. Even when there is plenty of moist wood, malnutrition may be caused by competition from the germinating spores of one's siblings. Poisoning by other fungal species, whose domain the spore has entered, is another threat. There are so many other ways to die young, and the probability of longevity too slim to calculate. This computation, however, is precisely what the mushroom has done. Its output of spores has been fine tuned by natural selection to maximize survival and limit wastage.

Mushrooms illustrate the Malthusian "perpetual struggle for room and food" with greater force than any animal. On a global basis, the total fertility rate for our species is 2.3 births per woman; the births per giant puffball, *Calvatia gigantea*, soar into the trillions (Plate 2). This astonishingly prolific mushroom is also a common species, like the blood-foot, but it inhabits pastures rather than forests. Despite its sedentary condition, the puffball doesn't have any obvious problems casting spores over its habitat. The merest gust will spill its powdery offspring, and raindrops send a fog of them into the air. Those trillions of spores are necessary, not to find fresh grassland, but, once deposited, to survive the trials endured by every fungal spore: unpredictable climate, predation, and competition. This is why meadows are never filled with puffballs, but instead are decorated, here and there in their soggiest spots, with white globes that flag their subterranean colonies.

A raindrop is all that some species require for germination; others have more refined physical or chemical needs. Giant puffball spores are particularly resistant to germination in the lab, with only one per thousand agreeing to grow in a Petri dish.[2] Experiments suggest that more will germinate in the presence of yeasts (single-celled fungi), which offers a glimpse of the complexity of a spore's natural existence. This intertwining of life cycles, with mushrooms reliant on yeasts, or insects, or even birds, may explain why the spores of so many fungi have never been germinated in the laboratory. These diverse interactions may involve exposure to foreign secretions, cohabitation within the same food source for the purpose of cooperative digestion, or entail greater intimacy such as the passage through the partner animal's digestive system. Examples of mutually supportive relationships between insects and mushroom-forming fungi will be discussed in Chapter 3.

Germination occurs with the emergence of one or more slender filaments, or germ tubes, from the spore (Fig. 1.1). Some spores swell before they germinate, while others show no obvious signs of activity prior to the process. The germ tube extends for a while and then branches behind its tip, producing a second interconnected filament. Both filaments continue to extend until a second branch grows from the first axis, then more, and the branches form branches, and a network of filaments emerges within a few hours. This is the young mycelium, a colony whose multiple tips expand the fungus in an ever-enlarging circle from the original spore sitting at its hub. This rapid development of a series of perfectly cylindrical tunnels whose liquid contents pulse toward their extending tips is a beautiful thing to watch under a microscope. My introduction to the mycelium's shape was provided by my dad, who explained that Alexander Fleming discovered the antibiotic penicillin when he noticed that the sandwich he was about to shove in his mouth

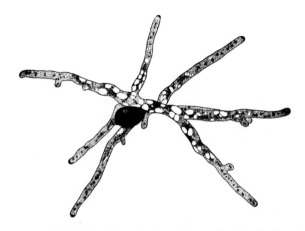

Figure 1.1. Day-old colony of an ink-cap mushroom that has developed from a single black spore.
Source: From A. H. R. Buller, *Researches on Fungi,* vol. 4 (London: Longmans, Green, 1931).

was covered with circles of blue mold. Dad embellished his story with the detail that Fleming's fungus had floated through an open window from a neighbor's filthy kitchen, but I was quite inspired that someone became a world-famous scientist simply by taking a close look at this lunch! (Forty years later, I remain traumatized by the memory of the teacher who told me, "It didn't happen quite like that, Nicholas," and then flogged me with his cane while singing our school hymn, "Onward Christian Soldiers").[3] Speaking of childhood again, the colony of branched filaments is the adolescence, of sorts, of the mushroom to come.

The first microscopists saw these filaments, or hyphae, in the seventeenth century. Marcello Malpighi, better known for his work on insect anatomy, offered the first illustration of these structures in his *Anatome Plantarum,* published in the 1670s.[4] The function of spores as fungal "seeds" was surmised a century before Malpighi but was not proven until experiments by the brilliant Florentine naturalist Pier

Antonio Micheli were published in 1729.[5] Micheli didn't observe germination, but he pictured spores and demonstrated that a dusting of them cast from one mushroom could spawn a new flush of the same type of fruit bodies in a leaf pile. The evident vitality of the fungi was a source of wonder for these pioneering investigators, and there was a great deal of confusion surrounding their affinity with other forms of life. Micheli held the widespread view that the fungi were simple kinds of plants, but others treated them as a curious branch of the animal kingdom. (Less anthropocentric investigators might regard the animals as a grotesque branch of the fungal kingdom.) In his *Micrographia*, Hooke described mushroom structure in the section on sponges, while Linnaeus wrote of animalcules arising from fungal spores and classified them in the genus *Chaos* under the worms (*Vermes*) in the twelfth edition of the *Systema Naturae*. This is interesting in light of the modern perspective, which considers the fungi as a sister group to the animals, with both related only distantly to the plants.

The first clear description of germination was published a century later by the French investigator Bénédict Prévost, who showed that spores of the smut fungus, *Tilletia caries*, caused the bunt or stinking smut in wheat.[6] Detailed descriptive work on germination followed in the 1870s, when Oscar Brefeld introduced pure culture techniques and used gelatin as a surface for growing fungal colonies.[7] By keeping his cultures free from contaminating molds, Brefeld was successful in following the development of ink-cap mushrooms of *Coprinopsis stercorea* all the way from single hyphae. Most mushrooms will not develop in this nonsexual fashion, as I'll explain soon, but the ink cap chosen by Brefeld is a handy onanist that can do everything on its own.

Experiments on spore germination were further pursued by an unexpected figure in Victorian mycology, a woman best known as an author and illustrator of children's books. Beatrix Potter—inventor of the mischievous Peter Rabbit—developed a keen interest in natural history during her childhood holidays in Scotland and the English Lake District, and this passion proved lifelong. She painted beautifully observed watercolors of mushrooms that were used, posthumously, to illustrate an influential book on mushrooms.[8] In addition, Potter worked with a microscope and, as her interest in fungi grew in the 1890s, she began wrestling with questions about the development of lichens and the life cycles of mushrooms. She thought that lichens might be formed by fungi capable of generating their own chlorophyll-containing cells. Hoping, perhaps, to document this transformation, Potter carried out experiments on spore germination that echoed earlier studies by Brefeld. One of the organisms she studied formed little discs, or crusts, on the surface of tree trunks and on branches. Succeeding in germinating its large spiny spores, she may have believed that she was witnessing the earliest stages of lichen development. But these investigations ceased when she shared her findings with George Murray, Keeper of Botany at the Natural History Museum in London, who explained that her "lichen" was a fungus. The orange discs of *Aleurodiscus amorphus* certainly bear superficial resemblance to foliose or crustose lichens, but relatives of this fungus form conventional umbrella-shaped mushrooms and lack the algal partner of these symbioses. Potter also visited Kew to discuss her research, but she was dismissed by its pompous director. She persisted with her work, however, and seems to have parlayed her experience with *Aleurodiscus* into a wider exploration of spore germination among other mushrooms. She prepared a paper on these experiments for the Linnean Society, then withdrew the manuscript after an unenthusiastic airing at a meeting and abandoned her research. Potter was, nevertheless, a pioneering mycologist, one whose intelligence and inquisitiveness might have been channeled into a career in science had she possessed the Y chromosome required for most Victorian professions. Fortunately, her considerable artistic talents gave her other outlets for her ambition.

The transition from spores to colonies to mushrooms is a developmental journey that remains surprisingly mysterious. Since Brefeld and Potter, mycologists have learned a great deal about the processes that occur when spores germinate, and when colonies expand, but we are a long way from a compelling explanation of the cooperative interactions between individual cells that result in the formation of a functional mushroom. Research on development within an evolutionary context, known as "evo-devo," is among the most vibrant and successful fields of modern biology. Roundworms and fruit flies are favorites for evo-devo studies. These animals contain organs with functions analogous to human viscera, including primitive kidneys, intestines, sex organs, and so on, and we know a lot about how their anatomy is assembled. A mushroom is a good deal simpler in structure: it is a single organ formed from a single type of cell. This simplicity belies its intractability as a research subject. I'll tell you what we have learned so far, and outline, in the parlance of the retired American military genius Donald Rumsfeld, the "known unknowns," or, what we know we don't know.

Colonies that support mushrooms can be very small, occupying a damp twig, or very large, invading an enormous territory of forest soil. The current world champion is a colony of *Armillaria ostoyae*, one of the species referred to as a honey mushroom, that has populated 2,400 acres, or 10 square kilometers, of the Malheur National Forest in Oregon.[9] This fungus spreads by means of rhizomorphs, root-like structures that develop from scores of intermingling hyphae and bear some resemblance to mushroom stems. These are the blackened and often flattened "bootlaces" that can be found in woodland soil and under the bark of decaying trees. When hyphae grow in this cooperative fashion, they allow the fungus to expand at much faster rates than by finely dissected colonies of individual hyphae. By piping their own water supply toward their tips, they can grow across dry soil. A lot of the wood-decay fungi in forests produce rhizomorphs; they are a vital accessory to the hyphae that perform the feeding activities of the fungus.

As Brefeld showed, spores germinate with the protrusion of hyphal tips, usually one per spore, sometimes more. Hyphal elongation and branching shape a colony whose centrifugal expansion creates a network in which every scrap of territory can be probed by a feeding hyphal tip (Fig. 1.2). The pattern resembles the veins in a leaf, or the blood vessels in an animal. Each of these networks offers an efficient way to permeate a particular volume with tubes. Some fungal colonies engage in more frequent branching than others, and these branches can fuse to increase connectivity between different parts of the organism. Colonies of wood-decay fungi grown in wet sand in the lab look quite diffuse, forming bundles of hyphae

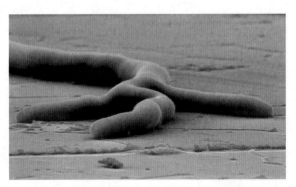

Figure 1.2. Scanning electron micrograph of hyphal tips growing over solid surface. These are the feeding structures common to all fungi.
Source: Photograph courtesy of Geoffrey Gadd, University of Dundee.

called cords (similar to rhizomorphs) separated by a few unbundled hyphae. This hungry colony enlarges over the desert, without changing its overall appearance, until one region encounters a wood block. When this happens, the fungus responds by concentrating growth toward the food, creating cords that connect directly to the wood and abandoning hyphae farther away. In the absence of any sophisticated sniffing system for finding wood, the fungus fans out in all directions, wagering that it will hit something nutritious at its periphery if it keeps growing long enough. A flawless illustration of this would be furnished by releasing a group of famished teenagers in an unfamiliar city and sending them off on all compass points with the sole instruction that they call their friends' cell phones if they find themselves under the Golden Arches. Most of them could be retrieved from the same McDonald's after a few hours of listless wandering.

Hyphae that form the colonies of mushroom-forming fungi are compartmentalized into short segments by cross-walls called septa. When viewed under a microscope, this gives hyphae the appearance of ladders with widely spaced rungs. The middle of each septum is perforated by a valve that allows for the flow of cytoplasm from one compartment to the next when it is open. Each compartment can be regarded as a cell, although it might be equally valid to consider that all of the interconnected compartments represent a single cell with lots of nuclei. (How many angels can dance on the point of a needle?) Colonies that develop from single spores have one nucleus per compartment. These colonies are called monokaryons, or homokaryons, referring to their solitary nuclei. In the textbook description of the mushroom life cycle, two of these colonies fuse to form a new type of colony, called a dikaryon, in which each compartment contains two nuclei—one derived from each of the original mates (Fig. 1.3). The dikaryon is the colony from which

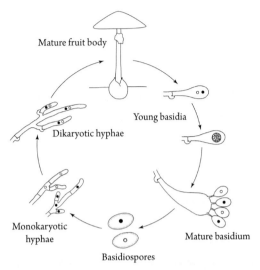

Figure 1.3. The basidiomycete life cycle. Basidiospores germinate to form colonies of monokaryotic hyphae containing nuclei of a single mating type. Compatible monokaryons merge and produce a dikaryon from which the fruit body develops. Nuclei of two mating types fuse within basidia on the gill surfaces; the fusion nucleus undergoes meiosis, and each of the four nuclei resulting from this division is packaged into a spore.

Source: Illustration includes drawings adapted from H. J. Brodie, *The Bird's Nest Fungi* (Toronto: University of Toronto Press, 1975), with permission.

the mushroom develops. Each time a new compartment forms in the dikaryon, it must be furnished with copies of each of the nuclei bequeathed by the pair of parental monokaryons. This involves some shuffling of dividing nuclei around the new septum, which is achieved by the production of a little hooked branch called a clamp connection. These are visible as bumps on the surface of the septa in the dikaryon.

There are exceptions to this cycle, including the formation of mushrooms by colonies derived from individual spores (such as the aforementioned ink cap studied by Brefeld) and the production of mosaic mushrooms by multiple partners. The majority of species, however, require sex between two consenting colonies. Experimental pairings of spores captured from single mushrooms provide valuable insight into the underlying genetic controls. In most cases, only one-fourth of these sibling crosses are successful, leading to the formation of a dikaryon; three-fourths of the time—the mushrooms being more sophisticated than European royalty—the pairings fail. Outcrossing is favored, for all of the good reasons that limit inbreeding elsewhere in nature. But while the Pope insists that all of humanity is ordained heterosexual, Kingdom Fungi have taken a more catholic approach to gender. A single mushroom species can embrace tens of thousands of genetically distinct sexes, and almost all of them can, and do, mate with one another. "Male" and "female" are meaningless. As long as one doesn't try to have sex with a nest-mate, cell fusion is sanctioned.[10] The reason for this libertinism may be that the chance of meeting another colony of one's species is quite limited, due to the prevalence of infant mortality among mushrooms discussed earlier. So when a hypha touches a hypha in the moist darkness of the soil, cell walls dissolve, fluids merge, and nuclei mingle.

German and French scientists using the latest microscope techniques made most of the advances in understanding fungal development in the nineteenth century. Oscar Brefeld was one of the central players, though he isn't as well known as his mentor, Heinrich Anton de Bary, whose 1866 textbook, *Morphologie und Physiologie de Pilze*, marked the beginning of modern mycology.[11] Their French contemporaries, the brothers Louis-Réne and Charles Tulasne, discovered that single species of fungi could form different kinds of spores, and they presented their findings in exquisitely illustrated folios.[12] The sexual behavior of the fungi was a crucial topic of exploration by the major practitioners of mycology in the nineteenth century, and wherever the curtains were opened, the mechanics seemed to involve the gentle fusion of colonies rather than the semen-on-eggs recipe for reproducing animals. The mushroom life cycle proved difficult to crack and it remained an enigma until World War I, due, in part, to the misdirected imagination of an amateur mycologist in England called Worthington G. Smith (Fig. 1.4a). Smith claimed that his relentless microscopic observation revealed that mushrooms dropped packets of sperm cells onto the soil that ejaculated over their spores. The effort involved in apprehending the nonexistent sperm cells is evident from his description: *At first it requires long and patient observation to make out the form of these bodies satisfactorily, but when the peculiar shape is once comprehended, there is little difficulty in correctly seeing their characteristic form.*[13]

The most likely explanation for Smith's error is that he confused contaminating protists, single-celled organisms with hairlike cilia, for mushroom sperm. This conclusion is supported by

Figure 1.4. British mycologists. (a) Worthington G. Smith (1835–1917), eccentric mycologist and archaeologist. (b) Elsie Maud Wakefield (1886–1972), graduate student who showed necessity for sex between colonies to produce mushrooms. *Source:* (a) Photograph from The Natural History Museum, London, with permission. (b) From C. G. Lloyd, *Mycological Notes* 7 (1924).

his admission that he added the "expressed juice of horse dung," hardly the cleanest of fluids, to keep his microscope preparations hydrated.

From a field of strong competitors, it seems fair to judge Worthington Smith as one of the most colorful figures in British mycology. Smith trained as an architect but became a celebrated illustrator of fungi, as well as an influential archaeologist. He said that he adopted the study of fungi "as a mental exercise," sometime after poisoning himself and his family by eating *Entoloma sinuatum*. Smith had mistaken this for an edible species and, adding to the unsavoriness of the story, kept the mushrooms under a glass bell for two days before cooking them in butter. After lunch, he set off from his home in Kentish Town for the city. Waiting for the train, he was "overtaken by a strange, nervous, gloomy, low-spirited feeling, quite new to me," then "a severe headache added its charms to my feelings." Stomach pains developed on the train and visual hallucinations at his destination. Returning home, he found his wife and daughter weak from vomiting and, overcome with drowsiness, Smith slept for twelve hours, dreaming of "toadstools...advancing and retreating, increasing in size and diminishing in an endless maze... poisoned children, dead fathers and mothers." He detailed the experience in an article published in the *Journal of Botany* and, in 1867, published a guide to mushroom identification.[14]

The befuddled picture of mushroom sexuality bequeathed by nineteenth-century science was swept away, finally, by Elsie Maud Wakefield, a twenty-three-year-old Oxford graduate who was studying in Munich (Fig. 1.4b). Evidence that mating was necessary to produce mushrooms emerged from her experiments with colonies produced from single spores: certain crosses resulted in fruiting, while others remained barren.[15] Wakefield was a pioneering scientist, one of the first women to become a professional mycologist, and she served as the Head of Mycology at Kew for forty years. Her importance in this chapter derives from her liberation of the mushroom life cycle from Worthington Smith's semen. After colonies merge, their commingled nuclei serve as gametes but delay fusing until the mushroom is mature. The pairs of nuclei remain partnered, within touching distance, in each compartment of the dikaryon for days, months, or even years. This extended foreplay is one of many characteristics that set the mushroom-forming fungi apart from the rest of life on earth. By committing early, I suppose, the couple can grow and feed together, and then share in the formation of mushrooms for dispersing their offspring. The final act of nuclear fusion occurs only in the cells, called basidia, that generate the spores on the gills.

The emergence of a mushroom from the colony of feeding filaments begins with a knot of hyphae. As this pinhead-sized congregation of cells enlarges, the stem, cap, and gills become visible, priming the developing embryo, or button, for rapid expansion into the mature reproductive platform as soon as environmental conditions are right (Fig. 1.5).

As I mentioned earlier, we know very little about how any of this happens. All animals share a catalog of genes that determine the positions where heads and tails and all of the stuff in the middle develop. Different versions of these genes, with names like *Hedgehog* and *Notch*, encode proteins that participate in signaling pathways that specified, when you were an embryo, that your anus would be planted toward your tail rather than the middle of your forehead. At best, the effects of gene mutations predicate gross unpopularity outside a circus tent or jar of formaldehyde. Because these kinds of developmental genes are ubiquitous among animals, it seems sensible to look for related genes, or homologs, that might play similar roles in determining the formation of caps and stems in mushrooms.

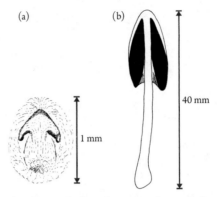

Figure 1.5. Development of the ink-cap mushroom *Coprinopsis cinerea*. (a) Primordium showing miniature cap and stem surrounded by protective hyphae. (b) Slice through mature fruit body that expands from the primordium in a few hours.

Source: Based on images in D. M. Moore, *Fungal Morphogenesis* (Cambridge: Cambridge University Press, 1998).

Exhaustive searches of fungal genomes, however, find that there are no such homologs in a mushroom.[16] Mushrooms hear a different drummer.[17]

Computer simulations are effective at generating virtual mushrooms from groups of filaments whose behavior is governed by a handful of rules.[18] These rules include the degree to which neighboring filaments attract or repel one another as they extend, the frequency of branching, the angles at which those branches grow, and the gravitational response of all of the growing tips. The power of the model lies in the fact that so few rules can specify a mushroom. (This is an application of Occam's razor in computer modeling: "Plurality should not be posited without necessity.") For instance, if we specified the behavior of each filament separately, then the virtual mushroom would tell us nothing more than a painting or a photograph of the real thing, but what the computer simulations show is that this kind of manipulation isn't necessary. By controlling a few parameters and applying these to all of the filaments at once, and then changing them and reapplying to all of the filaments, a beautiful cyberbolete can be grown (Fig. 1.6). This is an important discovery, because it means that the apparent complexity one sees in the woods, or in the pages of a mushroom guidebook, may emerge from a relatively simple set of controls.

The computer simulations also hint at the reason that the kinds of developmental genes ubiquitous among animals are absent in the fungi. According to the models, a developmental clock dictating the expression of successive waves of cell attraction and repulsion might be sufficient to shape everything from a mushroom with delicate gills to a fat bracket sticking out of a dying tree. Having advanced this possibility, however, investigators still need to identify the cell biological mechanisms that enable hyphae to sense the position of their neighbors (for one cell to grow away from its neighbor, it must be able to sense its propinquity), control branching, and perceive gravity. And, to indicate the enormity of the "known unknowns," we are nowhere close to pinpointing the genes that distinguish the fruit bodies of the 16,000 species of mushroom from one another. Generation after generation, with unwavering

Figure 1.6. Computer-simulated mushroom primordia.
Source: From A. Meškauskas, L. J. McNulty, and D. Moore, *Mycological Research* 108, 341–353 (2004), with permission.

fidelity, colonies of scarlet, parrot, lemon, olive, scented, stinking, ivory, and vermillion waxcaps (species of *Hygrocybe*) form their own versions of thick-gilled mushrooms. Some of the names of these mushrooms refer to variations in color or odor, but the differences go much deeper. The shapes of the fruit bodies are highly distinctive, from the pointed cap of the witch's hat (*Hygrocybe conica*, plate 3), to the flatter form of the lemon waxcap (*Hygrocybe chlorophana*), and the slimy bells of their relative, the parrot waxcap (*Hygrocybe psittacina*). Beneath the mushroom cap, there are variations in gill thickness and spacing that are patented by each species, along with differences in the shape and size of the cells that project from the gill surfaces and of the spores whose production is the raison d'être of the entire organ.

Cells called basidia form at the ends of hyphae whose tips stop growing at the gill surface. Like the billions of other compartments within the flesh of the mushroom, the young basidia contain copies of the pair of nuclei derived from the parent colonies. These fuse and then undergo meiosis (the dividing mechanism that creates eggs and sperm in animals) to produce four genetically distinct nuclei, each of which is packaged into a spore. The mature basidium looks a bit like a cow udder with a quartet of spores arranged on the teats. (Spores and basidia take center stage in the next chapter.) Once they escape from the mushroom, these spores populate the invisible biology of the air and their deposition in a suitable place completes the fungal life cycle. Spores, colonies, mated colonies, mushrooms, and more spores.

Sunlight triggers some of the steps in mushroom formation, including the initiation process and the formation of spores, but it does not dictate the orientation of a mushroom cap in the way that light controls plant growth. After all, lacking the ability to power sugar production by absorbing photons, fungi have evolved to feed in darkness on the fruits of plant photosynthesis. Instead, gravity is the environmental signal of paramount importance to a mushroom. The reason for this is apparent when we remember that mushrooms are platforms for spore dispersal. Once the spores are discharged from the gills, they fall vertically from the bottom of the cap and are dispersed by the airflow swirling around the fruit body. If the mushroom doesn't develop in an upright position, its gills pointing straight down, the spores will never escape and the fungus has no chance of sending its genes into the always uncertain future. Gravity is everything for a mushroom. More on this in the next chapter, but the evidence for gravitationally inspired growth is displayed in the arrangement of the spore-producing tissues in every mushroom. The precise arrangement of the gills under the cap can be examined by looking at a mushroom in a grocery store—they are formed in this manner because the cultivated mushroom takes its cues from gravity. The stem of the mushroom is similarly sensitive to gravity and the stem of a developing mushroom displaced horizontally will embark upon a right-angled turn to keep its gills pointing down. Mushrooms grown on the Space Shuttle become disoriented and form twisted stems as they "look" for the center of the earth.[19] Such cruelty is, sadly, an unpleasant part of the space program as any primate, aside from the ones with military haircuts, will testify.

With the exception of the cells that form the spores on the gill surface, all of the components of a mushroom are capable of abandoning their vocation within the fruit body and seeding a new colony. Hyphae cut from a mushroom cap or stem will fashion a feeding colony if they are placed on agar in a culture dish. This transformation is probably a rare event in nature, but the fact that the cells in a mushroom never give up their developmental flexibility is another of those remarkable features of the fungi that justify their distinction as a separate kingdom of life. Almost every cell in a mushroom is a stem cell.[20] Millions of them run up and down the stem and millions point sideways in the expanded cap; some form spherical compartments in the flesh of the gills, others (called cystidia) poke from the gill surface and form French-tickler tips. Position seems to be everything.

The mechanical process of expansion plays an important role in determining hyphal orientation, because the cells are yanked into position as the embryo inflates. The term "inflation" is appropriate for mushroom development because the dramatic overnight appearance of the fruit body on a lawn, or anywhere else, is not associated with an increase in the number of cells.[21] The process is hydraulic, involving the uptake of water into all of the preexisting, preorganized cells from the youngest stages of fruit-body development. For this to occur, the cell walls of the hyphae loosen and water influx occurs passively by osmosis. This is a beautifully simple mechanism in physiological terms, nothing like the growth and differentiation entailed in human embryogenesis. Mushroom inflation involves limited gene expression and finishes in a few hours. Because the walls of the hyphae in the mushroom do not expand indefinitely, they become pressurized by this water influx. This pressure, called turgor, induces tension between the different tissues in the fruit body, causing the stem to elongate and the cap to expand outwards, displaying the gills. Any gravitationally urged curvature of the stem is controlled by differential relaxation among the hyphae that occupy the outermost rind of the stem, while the innermost cells continue to produce the elongating thrust. The exertion of as much as one atmosphere of this pressure also powers the emergence of the fungus from soil or rotting wood.[22] In the urban environment, this allows fungi to lift paving slabs and crack asphalt. In the indoor environment, a cluster of mushrooms beneath your seat cushion would exert sufficient force to raise you, the cat sleeping on your lap, and your brandy balloon a few inches above your leather armchair.[23]

By seeking to paint a picture of mushroom development in fairly broad brushstrokes, this chapter has described the formation of an average-looking gilled mushroom. There are, however, all manner of variations on this model. In species of *Amanita*, including the lethal death cap, the button stage is wrapped in a continuous layer of tissue called the universal veil that is torn apart as the mushroom expands. This tissue appears as remnants in the form of spots, or scales, on the cap, and cup, or volva, at the base of the stem (Fig. 1.7). A second veil, called the partial veil, covers the bottom edge of the gills and this splits away from the outer edge of the expanding cap and hangs down as a ring on the stem. I have focused here on mushrooms with gills, but mushrooms also fold their spore-producing tissues over ridges beneath their caps, or teeth, or within the inner surface of tubes. Other species display their spores on exposed surfaces, forming

Figure 1.7. Origin of the mushroom volva and ring. (a) Emergence of *Amanita phalloides* showing origin of basal cup, or volva, from torn universal veil that wrapped around the entire mushroom. (b) Enormous floppy ring on stem of *Agaricus silvicola* hanging beneath the gills that it covered as a partial veil.

Source: (a) From R. D. de la Rivière, *Le Poison des Amanites Mortelles* (Paris: Masson, 1933), (b) Author's photograph.

mushrooms that resemble little corals. Stinkhorns and cage fungi smear spores in odorous, insect-attracting paste on phallic heads or over the bars of cages. Puffballs and earth stars produce their spores within the chambers of their labyrinthine innards, while bird's nest fungi and the artillery fungus fashion packets of spores that resemble miniature puffballs. Despite this astonishing diversity of forms, all fruit bodies begin life as a primordial knot of hyphae that shows rapid, hydraulically powered expansion. Unfortunately little is known about the environmental cues that initiate this amazing process.

Temperature and rainfall are the most obvious signals that may dictate mushroom emergence. The appearance of mushrooms after rain, rather than in the dead of winter, is a matter of common observation. But it's not as simple as: rain + warmth = fruiting. A mushroom unfurling its gills in the woods on a rainy morning in September will also pop up on the same day many miles away in an island of trees in the middle of farmland. This precise calendar is a feature of many species. For mushrooms whose colonies are associated with tree roots—mycorrhizal partners or destructive parasites—the timing may be controlled partly by the physiology of the host. Yet species that fruit on logs do the same thing, developing across a wide geographic area during a single week each year. This suggests that emergence may be facilitated by moisture but allowable only when a multitude of other variables are in place, including permissive soil temperature, changes in day length, and the pulse of nutrients supplied by leaf fall in temperate regions.

Mushroom colonies have complex dietary requirements. Nitrogen is a critical element because it is in short supply within many of the food sources preferred by fungi, ranging, for example, from one part in one hundred to less than one part in one thousand in wood. Estimates suggest that a one-kilogram bracket fungus needs to harvest all of the nitrogen from 14 kilograms of timber to support its annual spore production. This illustrates why colonies of some species must spread over large territories before producing mushrooms. Colonies that live for hundreds or even thousands of years can afford to be sparing in their annual investment in spore production, shedding some of their gains while maintaining a healthy feeding colony within the forest soil. A radically different strategy is the approach taken by a coprophilous fungus that lives and dies in a steaming mound of elephant dung. Things are good for a while, but before long all of the calories in this beetle-riddled monument to defecatory excess will be gone and a fresh delivery in the same spot unlikely. The individual colony cannot travel beyond the dung and the only chance for sending its genes into the future lies in packaging spores and releasing them into the wind. It makes sense, therefore, for this colony to load as much of its resources as possible into spores and to disperse them in search of fresh dung.

Not a comfortable bedtime story, is it? The fungus is like a hopeful parent, up early in the morning to send the children off with their lunch boxes into a world of tremendous uncertainty … and the kids can never return and Mummy shrivels to death before sundown. Oh Darwin, you were a wicked man! The problem with this metaphor is that the notion of the individual, something that seems so obvious when thinking about animals, is more complex for a fungus. That big thing swimming off Cape Cod is a whale and that other big thing snoring in the armchair again is a professor. For a fungus, the mushroom is only the most visible part of the microorganism whose colony spreads underground. The individual fungus is the colony *and* all of its mushrooms. You can estimate the size of the individual by sampling the colony at various points and checking the identity of the filaments by amplifying their genes, but it is impossible to tell how much of the woodland colony is shifted to the surface in the form of mushrooms. Studies of fungi in cultures make this task slightly easier. The simple answer is that a good deal of the colony is shifted to the surface in the form of mushrooms by mobilizing nutrients from distant parts of the colony toward a series of foci from which the fruit bodies develop.

A Swiss study showed that the number of mushrooms produced by up to 194 different species peaked in response to abundant rainfall and that cooler temperatures in July and August predicted an early beginning to the mushroom season.[24] Detailed studies of historical fruiting patterns have shown that the calendar for fungal reproduction has shifted in recent decades. Rush Limbaugh, an American radio talk show host, has explained, "Despite the hysterics of a few pseudo-scientists, there is no reason to believe in global warming."[25] Mushrooms hold a different viewpoint. In southern England, for example, a study of tens of thousands of records of fruiting showed that the duration of the fall mushroom season has more than doubled since the 1950s.[26] The behavior of the fungi correlates with warmer temperatures in August and more rain in October. In Norway, fruiting has been delayed by an average of two weeks in the last 60 years, with particularly warm weather in fall and winter postponing fruiting in the same year and in the following year. The reason for the apparent stretching of the mushroom season in England and its compression in Scandinavia is not known, but such dramatic effects on fungal reproduction add to the melange of foreboding indicators about our changing climate. More alarming than changes in the fall fruiting calendar, perhaps, is the finding that some species have begun to fruit in the spring *and* in the fall. The effect is most pronounced among wood-decay basidiomycetes, which suggests that decomposition is accelerating. The ecological consequences of these changes are likely to be profound. But one must remember, according to Mr. Limbaugh and colleagues, climate change is a hoax.

Dismissal of rationality in favor of superstition and wishful thinking has been an enduring hallmark of humanity; we are a gullible species, predisposed to looking for simple answers to complex questions, and finding witches, ghosts, and gods at the merest provocation. It is not surprising, therefore, that mushrooms have been linked to the occult for millennia. The hallucinatory properties of a handful of species has led to their worship (Chapter 7), and the toxicity of others to vilification in folklore (Chapter 6), but their fickle behavior and sudden erections have surely encouraged these supernatural associations. While I don't have much patience for the supernatural, I am awestruck, sometimes overwhelmed, by the sight of a ring of fresh mushrooms in a dewy meadow, huge boletes protruding from wet banks of forest soil, or the flash of pyrotechnic yellow among rotting logs that advertises the first sulfur shelf, *Laetiporus sulphureus*, of the year. This is an expression of ludicrous sensitivity rather than evidence of spirituality, but perhaps they are the same thing. I have a recurring dream in which I find myself in a magical garden, a moss-carpeted, pullulating Eden, where the mere thought of a mushroom is rewarded by its immediate appearance.

I have nightmared too, of a nuclear holocaust, watched the mushroom clouds roar on my unconscious horizon, and segued, not surprisingly, to their living mimics, transforming the apocalypse into a hallucinatory foray beneath towering fungi. Their colonies have tunneled, metaphorically, throughout my brain. I know that entomologists, bryologists, and any-other-ologists are similarly excited by their chosen slices of biodiversity, but there is something particularly strange about the fungal kingdom, something alien to our sense of how the rest of life is arranged. Mycology is a rare obsession, compared, for example, with astronomy or birdwatching; but there are many thousands of fellow worshipers, I hope, for whom the mushroom-scented forest is a secular cathedral. Rather than diminishing the magic, the dismissal of fairies and elves, this scientific "unweaving of the rainbow," intensifies the brilliance of nature's masterpiece, the mushroom. And that is what this book is for.

Chapter 2

Gill Gymnastics

THE BEAUTIFUL MECHANISM OF MUSHROOM SPORE RELEASE

Breakfast is a fantasy for most of us, an opportunity that might, if we're lucky, be afforded by retirement; more often than not, we race into Starbucks while carbon dioxide trails from the car left running in the street. But imagine a different time, when morning began with a walk across a muddy yard, though the gate and up into the meadow to collect a basket of fresh field mushrooms; a time when coffee was poured from a pot heated on a wood-fired stove and the term "skinny macchiato" was reserved for your emaciated farmhand. The mushrooms glistened in rings upon the dew-drenched grass; plump stems and white caps bore thin-spoked wheels of chocolate brown gills. Brushed free of earth, these were cut and fried with bacon . . . breakfast would then be followed by a day of backbreaking farm labor, an accident with a scythe, and an infection in your buttocks that would see you into the grave before the month was out. I think I'm happier in the twenty-first century! Though I do long for those mushrooms.

Meadow mushrooms, fruit bodies of *Agaricus campestris*, were common in the farmland of my English childhood but have become a rarity. Too much fertilizer on the fields, perhaps, or maybe something more insidious and climate change-related is at work. This meadow fare may end up on the endangered species list before long, while their cultivated cousin, the white button mushroom, *Agaricus bisporus*, positively flourishes. Whole or sliced, fresh or canned, this fungus has spread across the globe. Yet, this snowy cultivar is a freak of nature, a mutant whose damaged gills sport half the spore production of its wild kin. As a mutation, this would be crippling in a meadow, where spore production and dispersal are the only reasons for the mushroom's existence. With its adopted role as a grocery item, though, the fungus is doing fine. Hundreds of thousands of tons of white button mushrooms are grown each year in the United States alone. Like other slaves of agriculture, this mushroom is a weakling in the wild but a champion on the farm.

Wild meadow mushrooms, by contrast, are extremely good at their job: a single fruit body can discharge 2.7 billion microscopic spores per day, or 31,000 spores per second. But if you look closely at a meadow mushroom—or at any other mushroom, for that matter—it doesn't seem to be doing anything, does it? It is the embodiment of sluggishness. Its emergence may have been impressive, but now that it's erect, the mushroom sits in the grass as the sun rises and the dew evaporates, waiting to be picked for the aforementioned farmer's last seated breakfast. It betrays no motion whatsoever. Or so we thought until the last century—looked at under a microscope, the gills of a mushroom come alive to reveal an Olympiad of gymnastic cells.

The scientist who began to unravel the complexity of mushroom behavior was an English gentleman named Arthur Henry Reginald Buller (1874–1944). Buller was, without any competition before or since, the greatest mycologist in history—the Einstein of the field. Einstein published his most important work in 1905—his *annus mirabilis*—when he was 26 years old; Buller, like most biologists, peaked a good deal later. The first volume of his *Researches on Fungi* was published midway through his life, at age 35, the year 1909 marking the beginning of decades of explosive productivity.[1] Another six volumes of the *Researches* followed, one published posthumously, and a miscellany of unpublished ideas languishes in notebooks in the library at Kew. Born in Birmingham, England, Buller moved to Canada in 1904 as a founding member of the science faculty at the University of Manitoba. There, he became obsessed with the mechanism that releases spores from mushrooms.

Spores form on cells called basidia that project horizontally from the vertical surfaces of the gills. The arrangement of spores on their basidia can be examined, quite easily, by excising a gill from any kind of mushroom, laying it flat on a microscope slide, and protecting it from immediate desiccation with a cover glass. Even at low magnification, the grouping of spores in quartets is apparent. This simple observation was first made by Micheli in the eighteenth century and published in his revolutionary work *Nova Plantarum Genera* (Fig. 2.1).[2] Micheli identified and named many species of fungi and experimented extensively on mushroom formation, discrediting the millennial belief in spontaneous generation more than a century before Louis Pasteur. Mushroom spores form in fours because fertilization occurs in the base of each basidium, with two nuclei fusing, then dividing by meiosis (see Fig. 1.3). Meiosis produces four nuclei, each with a single set of chromosomes, and each mushroom nucleus is packaged into a spore. The spores sit at the tips of pointed stalks, called sterigmata, that project from the basidium (Fig. 2.2).

Two hundred years after Micheli, Buller looked at spores using the same method, but he also studied them as they fell from slices of mushroom gills clamped in a special chamber. Using a customized horizontal microscope, he watched spores disappear from their basidia and saw others coming into view beyond the

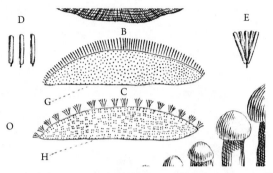

Figure 2.1. Detail from P. A. Micheli, *Nova Plantarum Genera* (Florence: Bernardi Paperinii, 1729), Plate 73, showing arrangement of spores on the gill surface in groups of four (H). The tufts on the edge of the gill have been variously interpreted as spores seen in profile, or as hairs. Micheli's discovery of the spore arrangement was forgotten for a century, during which mycologists published delusive illustrations of mushroom spores based upon careless observation.

gill, a short distance away, before floating slowly out of focus. The spores were being shot from the gill surface in astonishing numbers by some unknown mechanism, and they were moving very fast—the only evidence of their launch was their disappearance. Buller noted an important detail: in the seconds before each spore vanished, a tiny drop of fluid developed at its base (Fig. 2.2). He called it the "water-drop," and today we refer to it as Buller's drop. Buller guessed that what he saw was important, but never figured out why—it turns out the drop is critical to the mechanism of spore discharge.

The behavior of Buller's drop has recently been studied using high-speed video cameras.[3] Most feature films are captured at a rate of twenty-four individual images per second, and it would require no more than 100 frames to record, for example, Angelina Jolie falling off a camel headfirst into a steaming pile of excrement. Cameras running at this speed are certainly fast enough to show Angelina's

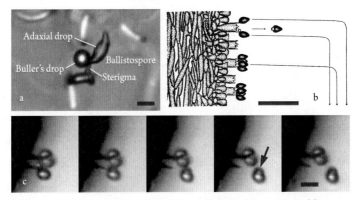

Figure 2.2. The process of spore discharge in basidiomycete fungi. (a) Spore of the stinking smut fungus *Tilletia caries* perched on its sterigma, showing Buller's drop and adaxial drop a few seconds before discharge. (b) Predicted trajectories of spores discharged from basidia on a mushroom gill illustrated by A. H. R. Buller in 1909. The fluid drop that powers discharge is shown at the base of the spore attached to the uppermost basidium, and is also carried on the discharged spore. (c) Successive images of spore discharge from a gill of the mushroom *Armillaria tabescens* from high-speed video recording captured at 50,000 frames per second. Buller's drop (arrowed) is carried with discharged spore. Scale bars, a, c, 10 μm, b, 50 μm.

Source: From J. L. Stolze-Rybczynski et al., *PLoS ONE* 4(1): e4163 doi:10.1371/journal.pone.0004163 (2009).

in-flight grimace, but they are useless for studying spore movement. Fungal launch mechanisms, and other microscopic movements, are much faster than gravitational tumbles, which is why cameras that grab 250,000 images per second (or more) are the instruments of choice.

The latest generation of ultra-high-speed cameras seems quite miraculous to me. They can churn away for hours, capturing a tremendous number of images every few seconds, continually emptying a buffer in the camera memory so it isn't overwhelmed. When the operator stops the camera, there is an archive of little files

(1 million captured in four seconds for the 250,000-images-per-second frame rate) that can be downloaded to a computer. Most of these files are not at all interesting: spore release occurs so swiftly that 999,950 or more of them can be deleted. Happily, the needle in the haystack, the few frames that show the movement, can be located quite easily using the computer. The difficulty lies in handling the fungus, collecting wild material from the woods or culturing it in the lab, judging when the mushroom is ready to fire its spores, and creating an environment in which it will do so under a microscope with bright illumination. In other words, the director is everything.

High-speed images of spores shooting out of gills show that the Buller's drop merges with the wet spore surface, shifting its position from the base of the spore toward its free end. This shift in mass occurs in about 1 millionth of a second and flips the spore off its perch (the sterigma) and into the air (Fig. 2.2). The reason that Buller's drop moves is quite simple. The drop forms from condensation of the damp air surrounding the spore. This air between the gills is kept humid by the continual evaporation of water from the mushroom's tissues. Water evaporates from most surfaces of the mushroom, but it collects on the base of the spore, on a little projection called the hilar appendix (Fig. 2.3). Mannitol and other sugars weep from the spore's appendix, causing the feverish recruitment of water molecules from the air to drive drop expansion. Once initiated, the drop grows for a few seconds until it reaches a critical radius that allows its curved surface to touch the adjacent part of the spore holding a second drop of fluid called the adaxial drop. When this happens, Buller's drop washes into the adaxial fluid as fusion lowers their combined surface tension, just as two raindrops on a window pane will snap together as soon as they make contact. The diagram in Fig. 2.3 shows how this

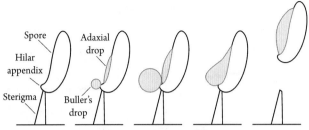

Figure 2.3. Drawing showing spore discharge process. Buller's drop and adaxial drop form via condensation of water on the spore surface, and their coalescence causes a rapid shift in the center of mass of the spore that is responsible for the launch.

Source: From J. L. Stolze-Rybczynski et al., *PLoS ONE* 4(1): e4163 doi:10.1371/journal.pone.0004163 (2009).

works. The physics of drop formation explains why this kind of spore release is restricted to humid conditions.

Drop motion catapults the mushroom spore into the air at a velocity of about 1 meter per second, or 3.6 kilometers per hour. This is quite slow, of course, comparable to the walking speed of a person in no hurry to get anywhere. For a microscopic particle, however, this speed is rather impressive—if the spore sustained this velocity for 1 second, it would travel a distance equal to 100,000 times its own length. A human moving at a comparable clip would be hurtling at 500 times the speed of sound.[4] The reason that fungal spores are shot at such high speeds is that air presents a tremendously viscous obstacle to the mobility of such small things. If spores were shot more slowly, they would barely separate from the gills. To reach these speeds, even for a few milliseconds, the spores are launched at astonishing accelerations. Drop movement propels mushroom spores from their sterigmata at accelerations of thousands or tens of thousands of *g*'s. These fast accelerations are due to the instantaneous nature of the launch. Unlike a departing airliner, which exhibits a steady increase in velocity when it trundles along the runway, or a rocket roaring from its launch pad, the fungal spore is static one moment, sitting on its sterigma, and 1 millionth of a second later it is moving through the air at maximum speed. The fastest launch I'm ever likely to experience will be in my car, which will go from 0 to 60 miles per hour (96.6 kilometers per hour) in 5.1 seconds, which is an acceleration of 5.3 g. This makes me feel like James Bond—or at least his more bookish, thin-haired brother—but the mushrooms are laughing as I whiz by. What my fungal critics should acknowledge (according to my therapist) is that their violent spore launches are also exemplars of humiliating deceleration. As soon as the spores start moving, their travel is slowed by air resistance, and they stall within a few spore lengths of the gill. Their flights are completely dominated by air viscosity and have negligible inertia compared to the black BMW driven by Professor Baldy Bond. Remember that mushroom spores are minuscule and that they experience air as a thick soup of gas molecules, and you will have grasped the major impediment to fungal motion and the reason for the elegant discharge mechanisms that have evolved in the last half-billion years.

Both faces of a mushroom gill are covered with basidia and shed spores. When Buller watched spore discharge using his horizontal microscope, he noticed that they were dragged to a halt in the air around the midline between the opposing gills. This limited throw is crucial, because it stops spores from crashing into the gill on the other side of the air space. If the viscous drag of air acted upon a baseball with the same intensity that it impedes the flight of a mushroom spore, you would see the pitched ball slow after an arm's length of motion, stop dead, and fall to the ground. I refer to this flight path as the Wile E. Coyote trajectory. What is tragic for the cartoon canid is successful for the mushrooms, because it enables them to shoot lots of spores from closely crowded gills, ensuring that they will stop quickly and fall out cleanly between the gills. In technical terms, this is described as a "****ing brilliant" mechanism.

The horizontal portion of the spore's flight lasts for no more than a few milliseconds; it spends far more time descending between the gills, a few seconds at least, before it clears the bottom of the mushroom cap and is swept away by air currents. In other words, the result of tens of thousands of drop movements every second on the gills of a meadow mushroom is a smoke of microscopic spores cascading from the cap. The magnitude of this release is usually invisible in daylight, but it can be seen by shining a flashlight or laser pointer beneath an active mushroom at night. The effect is dazzling—a blizzard of iridescent dust cascades through the light beam, each spore glinting for a moment before it falls out of view.

It takes a great deal of energy for a fungal colony to construct a mushroom and to make vast numbers of spores of a particular size and shape, but the spore discharge process is one of marvelous thriftiness. The mechanism, called ballistospory, is beautiful in its simplicity and economy. It relies solely upon water condensation and the passive movement of the resulting drops of fluid, and the only metabolic investment lies in the secretion of sugars onto the spore surface to drive drop formation. The majority of the 30,000 species of basidiomycete utilize this strategy. Ballistospory is thought to have evolved in the ancestors of the basidiomycetes because it doesn't occur in any of the other major groups of fungi.[5]

Nobody knows when the earliest mushroom relatives took to the evolutionary stage, but we can make some educated guesses. Exquisitely preserved mushrooms were found in 94-million-year-old amber, from the latter part of the Cretaceous, and older fossils that look like basidiomycetes have been dated to 300 million years ago.[6] The oldest fossils are remnants of hyphae with structures called clamp connections that are a diagnostic character for the basidiomycetes (Chapter 1). Genetic evidence locates the origin of the group way back toward the end of the Precambrian era, around 600 million years ago. The first basidiomycetes were probably quite simple in developmental terms. They didn't form mushrooms, nor any other type of fruit bodies, but grew as budding yeast cells or as colonies of filamentous hyphae and shed spores directly into the prehistoric air. It's worth considering the logic of this supposition for a moment, because it is easy to jump to conclusions about simple things begetting more complex things and the idea of some inevitable progress toward a fly agaric or an imperious human. In the case of the basidiomycetes, however, the idea of a simple progenitor—a yeast rather than a full-fledged mushroom—makes a great deal of sense. If we look at today's basidiomycetes that grow as yeasts, we find some species that do not use drop formation to launch their spores. They cause all manner of fungal mischief, including infecting humans (sometimes killing them), growing in maple syrup, and even producing dandruff. It is probable that these simple fungi evolved from ancestors that never learned the trick, but somewhere in the jumble of long-extinct yeasts was a species that developed the mechanism for shooting spores using a drop of fluid. A most persistent microbe, this species left behind its genes and its spore-launch trick as evidence in the rusts, smuts, and mushrooms of the twenty-first century.

Diversification of the basidiomycetes probably coincided with the development of land-dwelling plants in the Ordovician. Coevolution is likely because fungi need a food source, and plants would have afforded this: through their living tissues, for the earliest fungal parasites, and through their remains, for fungi decomposers. Fungi may also have infected or grown in the guts of invertebrates that fed on plants. Another possibility is that the early basidiomy-cetes lived on the sugary secretions from plant tissues, as do an unrelated group of fungi called "sooty molds."

Yeasts that fire their spores like mushrooms are a boon for researchers, because they will discharge their spores in naked, ungilled glory from the glistening surface of a culture dish. Rather than producing four spores per basidium like a mushroom, each of the ballistosporic yeasts' cells sheds a single spore. Nevertheless, these yeasts will cover a Petri dish in a few days and mist their lids with billions of spores. If the budding yeasts are arranged on the agar in a recognizable pattern, a letter for example, then a copy of this character is spattered onto the lid in the form of discharged spores. This phenomenon has earned them the name "mirror yeasts." In nature, the mirror yeasts act much the same way as they do in culture, although they fire their spores directly into the air. Like the nonbal-listosporic yeasts, these fungi grow on an amazing variety of mate-rials, including wet leaves and flower petals, wild mushrooms, the surfaces of appliances used to make cakes and candies, and within the tissues of patients with crippled immune defenses. Wherever they are exposed to moist air, they form their spores, recruit water vapor to produce Buller's drops, and launch themselves skyward. Their astonishing fecundity, ability to form spores without a mate, and undiscerning nutritional tastes explain why their spores are ubiquitous. It is difficult to take an air sample from anywhere on the planet and not find them.

Much the same can be said for the rusts and smuts that cause devastating diseases of cereal crops and other plants. These fungi do not form mushrooms of any kind, and they release their spores like the mirror yeasts (Fig. 2.2a). Buller studied the formation of "his" drop in the rusts and the smuts and recognized that the presence of the same mechanism he had documented in mushrooms indicated evolutionary affinity. In the yeasts, as in the rusts and smuts, the mechanism flings the spore over distances ranging from 0.5 to 1.5 millimeters, allowing them to clear the boundary layer of still air directly above the colony. These are the longest of the launches powered by drop movement. Compared with other spore discharge processes that have evolved among the fungi, the drop mechanism doesn't carry spores very far at all. Some of the lengthiest flights are driven by pressurized squirt guns that can shoot spore-filled balls called sporangia over distances greater than 2 meters. These squirt guns evolved in the zygomycete and ascomycete fungi, and they provide some of the most dramatic movements in the fungal kingdom.[7] The squirt gun with the greatest range is found in *Pilobolus*, a fungus that grows in herbivore dung. The fungus makes its way into this glorious all-you-can-eat buffet by sticking to grass blades until it is swallowed by a cow, an elephant, or another vegetarian. When the animal deposits its digested vegetables, the fungus luxuriates in the sudden burst of fresh air, dines on carbohydrates in the dung, pokes its crystalline stalks toward the sun, and produces millions of spores. Most herbivores prefer grazing on grass some distance from their own excrement (which doesn't seem unreasonable), and this explains why evolution has fashioned such a magnificent launch mechanism for *Pilobolus*. A high-speed video montage of this process, set to the *Anvil Chorus* from Verdi's *Il Trovatore* and posted on YouTube by my students, received 100,000 hits in its first couple of months in cyberspace and generated comments about fluid expulsion that cannot be printed in a book written for the enjoyment of innocent readers.

Pilobolus is an exceptional flyer. But unless you live in dung, such a lengthy flight may prove a waste of energy. So other squirt guns discharge spores over shorter distances: often a few centimeters, sometimes mere millimeters. The fungi are advantaged in these launches by traveling far beyond the stationary air close to the surfaces on which they are growing and reaching air currents that have the potential to carry their spores over great distances. Micheli was first to illustrate an extravagant manifestation of squirt gun activity in a tiny illustration in his 1729 book (Fig. 2.4). He showed a little cup fungus and the shower of spores above its surface. This "puffing" is caused by a fusillade of ejaculations from thousands of pressurized cells called asci. These asci line the interior of the cupped fruit body and mature in groups, such that thousands of them, sometimes hundreds of thousands, can expel their spores simultaneously in response to the appropriate trigger. Airflow activates puffing, probably by causing a dip in the humidity above the asci. If you find a cup fungus in the woods, gentle blowing over its surface will be rewarded with a puff of spores and, if your hearing is sufficiently sharp, a sizzling sound as the asci burst. All of the mature

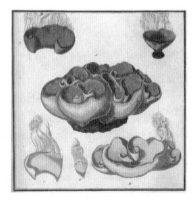

Figure 2.4. Mass discharge, or puffing, of ascospores by cup fungi. (a) Earliest illustration of puffing by P. A. Micheli in *Nova Plantarum Genera* (Florence: Bernardi Paperinii, 1729). (b) Eighteenth-century figure by P. Bulliard in *Histoire des champignons de la France, ou, Traité él émentaire renfermant dans un ordre méthodique les descriptions et les figures des champignons qui croissent naturellement en France* (Paris: Chez L'auteur, Barrois, Belin, Croullebois, Bazan, 1791).

asci do not discharge at precisely the same time; in a big cup fungus, like one of the brown discs produced by a *Peziza*, the puffing spreads from one side of the fruit body to the other. This happens because the sudden deflation of asci in one region of the cup destabilizes the adjacent asci, causing them to fire, and so on across the cup. This domino effect drives the puffing process for a couple of seconds. Following the puff, more asci mature, preparing the cup for the next salvo. There is mechanical advantage in discharging spores in this way, because the motion of a mass of spores displaces a cylinder of air above the cup, serving to reduce the drag upon the flock of spores so they travel farther.[8]

The drop mechanism is incapable of these magnificent displays: it never shoots spores very far. The fine-tuning of the discharge distance, down to fractions of 1 millimeter, is surprisingly important and provides deep insights into the biology of the basidiomycetes. A mushroom with gills separated by a distance of 0.2 millimeter would not be very successful if its spores were shot as far as those of a yeast. The optimal flight would be lengthy enough to clear the gill surface, but considerably shorter than 0.2 millimeter. As tough as things might be for gilled mushrooms, bracket fungi face even greater challenges. A tree-killing species called *Ganoderma applanatum* illustrates the problem (Fig. 2.5). The largest of its brown brackets are as big as the lids of trash cans, and groups of these monsters sometimes form on tree trunks, creating ladders. These fruit bodies can grow for decades, expanding downward and outward each year, producing a series of furrows and thinning toward their outer edges. The upper surface of the bracket is dry and crusty, but the underside is pure white and pricked with millions of tiny holes. These holes are the pores at the ends of narrow, spore-producing tubes. Each year, the bracket produces a fresh layer of tubes, which is reflected in the wrinkles visible on the upper surface. If you cut the bracket in half,

Figure 2.5. Massive brackets of the artist's fungus, *Ganoderma applanatum,* on rotting stump of ancient European beech in Oxfordshire, England. Pores on the white underside of the fruit body connect with 2-centimeter-long tubes with diameters between 0.1 and 0.2 millimeter. The importance of the vertical alignment of these tubes for the escape of spores discharged from the inner surface of the tubes is illustrated in the diagram; spore paths indicated by arrows.
Source: Diagram reproduced from A. H. R. Buller, *Researches on Fungi,* vol. 2 (London: Longmans, Green, 1922).

you can discern the age of the fruit body by counting the successive layers of tubes. The flesh between the pores is sensitive to bruising, and this is exploited as a natural etching board by people of a particular artistic bent, explaining the common name "artist's conk." Some of the artwork on old brackets is spectacularly detailed, but I am repelled by the idea of cracking a 50-year-old bracket from a tree and inscribing pictures of rutting deer (a common theme), the pope being attacked by a unicorn, or anything else. There is more to be gained by looking at the unblemished bracket on the tree. The storm of spores falling from these giant brackets is truly an amazing sight and well worth an evening trek into the woods. Ten spores fall from each tube every minute; there are 2 million tubes on the underside of a bracket the size of a notebook computer, so spore output scales to 30 billion spores per day and more than 5 trillion in the six months that the bracket is active each year.[9] Five trillion spores weigh about 1 kilogram.

Now to the mechanical challenge. The *Ganoderma* spore is 10 millionths of 1 meter in length (10 micrometers) and is shot into a tube with a diameter of as little as 100 millionths of 1 meter (0.1 millimeter). After discharge, the spore must fall down the tube for a distance of 20 millimeters, or 2,000 times its own length, before it escapes from its hole on the underside of the bracket. Imagine yourself as a spore: if you survive the acceleration at launch, you'll find yourself in a pipe with a diameter of 20 meters, which is quite wide, but then have to fall down the center of the pipe for a distance of 4 kilometers before reaching the open end. Gravity will take care of your descent—it will take about one minute if you plummet like a skydiver—but the slightest misalignment of the pipe and you'll crash into the wall. Some Glaswegian scientists tested this in the 1960s, not by leaping into mine shafts, but by tilting bracket fungi on a platform whose orientation could be adjusted in quarter-degree increments from the vertical.[10] They found that misalignment of a bracket of the birch polypore, *Piptoporus betulinus*, by a single degree reduced spore release by 30% and 4 degrees was catastrophic, almost eliminating spore emission from the tubes. The tubes of the birch polypore are shorter than those of the artist's fungus, so *Ganoderma* spores pile up inside its tubes if it is tilted by only one-tenth of 1 degree. Not surprisingly, these fungi are adept at sensing gravity, and tube development is controlled to achieve almost perfect alignment. This gravitropic behavior is apparent when a tree supporting a bracket crashes to the ground. If the fungus isn't crushed, the bracket will grow a new layer of tubes aligned in the revised downward direction. The gills and teeth that hang beneath the caps of other kinds of fruit bodies exhibit similar finesse in alignment, but there is a greater margin of error in most species. The artist's fungus is a truly remarkable organism.

The formation of thin tubes by bracket fungi, like the close packing of gills in other mushrooms, greatly increases the surface area for spore production relative to a fruit body whose underside is flat. There are plenty of examples of mushrooms with flattened spore-producing tissues, and we do not know whether gilled or poroid mushrooms developed first in the evolutionary history of the fungi. Both have certainly evolved more than once. If we look at the different forms of fruit body from a purely mathematical point of view, the formation of gills and tubes is an undeniably efficient way to organize spore production. A meadow mushroom with a 10-centimeter-diameter cap can support more than 1,200 square centimeters of gill surfaces, which is a 16-fold increase in area relative to a flat surface. This would seem to make the best use of the tremendous amount of energy invested in creating the stem and cap of a mushroom. How, though, is discharge distance attuned to the mission-appropriate distances demanded by variously spaced gills, different-sized tubes, and so on? This is something that has been a complete mystery until recently.

Let's begin by thinking about spore size. Spore size and discharge distance are related. This makes mechanical sense: larger spores travel farther than smaller ones if they are both launched at the same speed, due to air's viscous properties. Air acts as an increasingly powerful brake against the motion of tinier and tinier particles. With the same initial velocity, a pea will fly across the table at your dinner companion, whereas a carefully aimed pork chop can fell an inattentive waitress on the other side of the room before she scuttles into the kitchen. Spore size isn't everything, however. An equally important factor is the size of Buller's drop relative to the size of the spore. A bigger drop will always propel a spore farther than a smaller drop, because its movement causes a greater shift in the projectile's center of mass (Fig. 2.3). What seems to have happened during the evolution of all manner of mushrooms is that spore and drop size became fitted to the structure of the fruit body. As I mentioned earlier, spores of a rust shot directly into the air are big, form big drops, and travel more than 1 millimeter; spores of a mushroom with lots of tightly packed gills are smaller, have smaller drops, and do not travel so far; spores of a coral fungus with finely dissected branches are really tiny and have even tinier drops. The coral fungus faces the same problem as a gilled mushroom because its spores are ejected from all sides of its candelabra-shaped fruit body and can easily get lodged on an opposing branch. In both cases, a short flight is advantageous.

The way that mushrooms control the size of their Buller's drops has been studied for the last 200 years—though nobody was aware of it—as taxonomists collected, described, and named new species of fungi. Spore shape and size are among the many metrics that scientists have used to delineate fungal species. For descriptions of mushroom-forming basidiomycetes, spores are collected by placing the mushroom cap on some paper and allowing it to shed its spores for a few hours, creating a beautiful wheel pattern in which each spoke is formed by the accumulation of spores that fall between gills. This is called a spore print, and the color of the spores observed in this way is used as a diagnostic character, in much the same way as one might list the color of eggshells in a bird book. The taxonomists go much further than this, providing measurements of the microscopic dimensions of spores, describing their staining reactions to various chemicals, and detailing features of their surface architecture, such as the presence of spines and warts. The appearance of spores can be a useful character for discriminating between species and provides powerful clues about the relationships among mushrooms that look very different from one another.

One group of mushrooms, called the Russulales, comprises fruit bodies of all kinds, many with gills, others with teeth or tubes beneath their caps, some forming little dishes, and still others forming coral shapes (Plate 4). Throughout this range of mushroom shape and size, we find striking similarities among the spores; the prettiest are ornamented with warts, crests, or spines that can be connected to one another via a network of veins. We know that these similarities are not coincidental, or due to evolutionary convergence, because genetic comparisons of these fungi provide an independent and irrefutable measure of their evolutionary kinship. The morphology of spores in the genus *Russula* was documented in extraordinary detail in a 230-page book published by mycologist Richard Crawshay in 1930, titled (what else?) *The Spore Ornamentation of the Russulas* (Fig. 2.6). This is an example of an act of singularly sustained passion and unacknowledged dedication that marks so many careers in the field of taxonomy. Works like Crawshay's illustrate the overlap

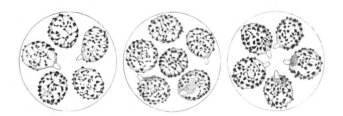

Figure 2.6. Basidiospores of *Russula* species illustrated by R. Crawshay, *The Spore Ornamentation of the Russulas* (London: Baillière, Tindall & Cox, 1930). Notice the patch on the surface of some of the spores adjacent to their projecting hilar appendices (shown as dots by Crawshay). This may function in separating the Buller's drop from the adaxial drop in the seconds before spore discharge.

between science and art. To pass a lifetime studying details of mushroom spores can be every bit as creative as one spent spreading paint over canvases, even if the final work of art is appreciated by no more than a handful of people.

There is, however, much more to fungal spores than their artistic merit. Lurking in their curves and folds and warts is a great deal of information about the way they work. Charles Darwin pondered this issue, albeit indirectly, when he discussed the intricate patterning on diatom shells with botanist George Thwaites in a letter written in 1860:

> …do you really suppose that for instance Diatomaceae were created beautiful that man, after millions of generations, should admire them through the microscope? I should attribute most of such structures to quite unknown laws of growth; and mere repetition of parts is to our eyes one main element of beauty. When any structure is of use (and I can show what curiously minute particulars are often of highest use), I can see with my prejudiced eyes no limit to the perfection of the coadaptations which could be effected by Natural Selection.[11]

Substitute "mushroom spores" for "Diatomaceae." Did Crawshay draw the random noise of evolution, or do spores with different shapes do different things? Observations with high-speed video suggest that details of spore architecture affect the mechanics of the discharge process. The reason that spore shape is so important has little, or nothing, to do with viscous drag and everything to do with Buller's drop. Spore shape seems to determine the maximum size attained by Buller's drop in the moments before it merges with the adaxial fluid and causes the launch. The mechanistic linkage is complicated: spore size determines drop size, drop size determines launch speed (bigger drops = faster launches), and launch speed, coupled with spore size, determines the distance that the spore moves through the air. If this is correct, two centuries of descriptive work by mycologists, including contributions like Crawshay's, offer an intimate profile of macroevolution in the fungi. Fungal species are defined, in part, by differences in the architecture of their spores, and this diversity of forms has been sculpted by natural selection.

Some changes in spore shape cause the drop to merge with the spore surface when it is very small, others when it has grown to a size that almost matches the spore itself. Our understanding of the linkage between spore architecture and Buller's drop size is quite limited at this time, and many of the fine details of spore structure are quite puzzling. Some spores have a special patch on their surface, just above the spot where the drop forms (Fig. 2.6). Warts and spines seem to be cleared from these patches and one possibility is that they serve to separate the fluid on the rest of the spore from the expanding Buller's drop until it reaches a critical size. Another possibility is that the patch holds the adaxial fluid in place. A century after Buller's pioneering research, we are only beginning to understand the link between these details of cellular architecture and the way that they control the launch of the spore.

The evolution of spore shape occurs in lockstep with the evolution of fruit bodies. A spore that's shot too far cannot escape from a mushroom with crowded gills; if the spores get stuck inside, the mushroom and its parent colony are doomed. As gills are pushed closer and closer together, increasing surface area for spore production, spore launches must be dampened to shorter and shorter distances. The shape and size of the fruit body are also critical to its success as a platform for spreading spores. Experiments in wind tunnels show that mushrooms with steeper, pointed caps slow the airflow beneath their caps. This may protect the spores from being blown back onto the bottom of the cap as soon as they emerge from their free fall. The cap may also act as an air conditioner, losing water over much of its surface to chill the surfaces on which the spores are formed. This makes physiological sense—any cooling of the mushroom will enhance the formation of the Buller's drops and promote spore discharge.[12]

The drop mechanism is a triumph of natural engineering, but many mushrooms have abandoned it. Among the Russulales, for example, some species never unfurl their gills, spending their lives underground as wrinkled nuggets of tissue resembling truffles. In a few of these aberrations the drop mechanism seems to be intact—if the fruit body is opened with a scalpel it will shed its spores and lay down an ugly print on paper. These fungi are interesting from an evolutionary perspective, because they are thought to be intermediate forms, mushrooms on their way to truffles. In other truffle-like species, the spore discharge trick has been lost entirely, and animals spread their spores by consuming the whole fruit body.

Stinkhorns, cage fungi, and their allies have also lost the drop mechanism in favor of smelling badly, but not to the flies that disperse their spores (Plate 5). Other mushrooms of this nonballistosporic omnium-gatherum include the puffballs, whose fruit bodies act like bellows, collapsing upon a raindrop's impact and spritzing clouds of spores into the air. Earth-stars and bird's nest fungi also make spectacular use of raindrops for spore discharge. Rain offers a source of abundant free energy for fungi. A small raindrop is 1 million times bigger and heavier than a spore; scaling up to human dimensions, a comparably small "raindrop" would weigh 100 kilotons and splatter poor Angelina with the force of 400 pounds of high explosive! Genetic comparisons show that puffballs evolved from gilled mushrooms, but, unlike their cousins, puffball spores are spherical, lack interesting surface features, and cannot form Buller's drops. This spherical form is seen in the spores of earth-stars and bird's nest fungi, too, suggesting that the loss of the usual asymmetry in spore shape in these species accompanied the alteration in dispersal mechanism.

These are the exceptions—most mushrooms behave as Buller first observed a century ago.[13] The discharge of all their spores has a major influence upon air quality. In instances of severe building contamination by the ballistosporic yeasts that I described earlier, studies have established that their spores can cause serious allergic illness. Outdoors, the astonishing numbers of spores released by mushrooms are reflected in their abundance in air samples. The "Mold Indexes" reported for most cities are dominated by the spores of mushrooms and their relatives at certain times of the year. Spores of the bracket fungus *Ganoderma* are often collected in air samples, which reflects this species' tremendous capacity for producing them. Atmospheric chemists studying the particulate matter above rainforests have found large amounts of sugars, including the compound mannitol, that they believe are hoisted aloft on the backs of mushroom spores in the form of their Buller's drops.[14] Using the measured concentrations in their air samples to estimate the global mass of dispersed basidiospores, they arrive at an astonishing figure of 17 megatons of spores per year. That's equivalent to the weight of more than 100 supertankers, or 100,000 blue whales. By acting as nuclei for water droplets and ice crystals, this haze of spores can shape precipitation patterns and cloud cover, and may even have a substantial influence on climate change.[15] Finishing this chapter on the 200th anniversary of Mr. Darwin's birth, it seems appropriate to acknowledge his 1859 maxim that "many more individuals of each species are born than can possibly survive." Mushroom spores offer a better illustration of this than anything else on the planet.

Chapter 3

Triumph of the Fungi

THE DIVERSITY AND FUNCTIONS OF MUSHROOM-FORMING FUNGI

Many enthusiasts for particular groups of living things share an experience of enlightenment, the light bulb above the head, when they are confronted by their beasts for the first time. Literal flashes of light from backyard fireflies might fertilize a lifelong passion for entomology, while the hammering of a pileated woodpecker or a television program on gorillas offers equally persuasive advertisements for the study of other animals. Mycologists can be initiated by a childhood walk in the woods and the sight of the overwhelming diversity of mushrooms, or, as in my case, an encounter with a single species. As a teenager, I spent a spell in the Air Training Corps, a youth organization supported by Britain's Ministry of Defense, which afforded occasional opportunities to fly in military aircraft, and, more frequently, participation in war games. One wet evening, racing through the woods on a map-reading exercise, my squad found itself at a crossroads, not knowing which path to take. A fly agaric poked from the grass at this junction. The bright red cap with white spots, the tall stem and drooping ring... I had no idea that things that grew in fairy tales grew, too, in nature. "What is that?" I said to a friend. "Jus an ol' grisette,"[1] he replied in his sweetly slurred accent of rural Oxfordshire, stabbed his finger at the map, and we slogged off into the mist beneath the conifers. I kept thinking about that mushroom. I can see it still today.

The fly agaric, *Amanita muscaria*, is *the* iconic fungus, the popular culture representative for the 16,000 species of mushroom that have been identified by mycologists (Plate 6). The formal name for the group, which is a taxonomic class, is the Agaricomycetes. This encompasses umbrella-shaped mushrooms and brackets with gills, spines, and tubes; others that bear spores on smooth surfaces or ripples; fruit bodies that form as flattened crusts upon tree trunks; puffballs; earth-stars; bird's nest fungi; phallic mushrooms; cage fungi; "false" truffles; a handful of species of artillery fungus; and an entire order whose fruit bodies feel like jelly (Fig. 3.1). On those golden occasions when many of these forms are encountered in the same location, the richness of color, shape, and size is breathtaking.

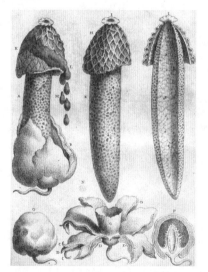

Figure 3.1. *Phallus impudicus*, the stinkhorn. An example of a mushroom-forming basidiomycete that utilizes the unconventional method of stinking and attracting flies for spore dispersal.

Source: From P. A. Micheli, *Nova Plantarum Genera* (Florence: Bernardi Paperinii, 1729).

Why are there so many different kinds—and colors—of mushroom? During my Oxfordshire childhood, I absorbed the idea that bright red mushrooms were poisonous and white ones more trustworthy. This might have made sense if mushroom colors evolved as anti-feedant devices, like the warning coloration of poisonous frogs, but this mycological racism has no validity. Contrary to the frog model, the intestinal distress provoked by fly agarics and some of the red *Russula* species is like a birthday kiss when compared to the liver- and kidney-demolishing chemicals within the pure white *Amanita* species called destroying angels. This point is underscored by statistical analysis showing that there exists no relationship between cap color and toxicity: irrespective of skin color, one-fourth of the species in a survey of 243 types of North American mushroom were identified as poisonous.[2] (There *is* a tenuous relationship between the odor of mushrooms and their toxicity, which I'll return to in Chapter 6.) With the putative link between color and toxicity disproved, there is no compelling explanation at the moment for the significance of mushroom coloration. This does not mean, of course, that Darwin was wrong and mushroom colors were intelligently designed 6,000 years ago for the delight of unborn mushroom enthusiasts. Differences in cap pigmentation may affect fruit body temperature and spore release, with cooler white mushrooms faring better in exposed locations where a red or brown cap would be warmed by light absorption.[3] Another possibility is that the red cap of the fly agaric may be one of those evolutionary spandrels, a by-product of fungal metabolism that confers no independent advantage to the species. Although cap color does not divine spore color, it is possible that the two properties may be linked through the biochemical circuitry activated during development. This conjecture does not get us very far, because we have no idea why spores come in different colors.

Anatomy and morphology usually provide more dependable information about an organism's evolutionary adaptations than color. Hummingbirds and albatrosses are avian dinosaurs whose physiques are beautifully adapted for hovering instead of soaring. Similarly, natural selection has sculpted an astonishing variety of insects that exploit different ecological opportunities. A blood-sucking mosquito requires mouth parts that are quite different from the jaws of an antlion, which grabs its prey at the bottom of a slip-pery sand-pit trap. Variations in the size and shape of mushrooms also make intuitive sense in terms of their adaptive value. A large, flat surface area of fertile tissue produces lots of spores, gills increase this surface area, and thin tubes are even better (Chapter 2). There are various ways of organizing these tissues, supporting gills underneath the caps of a few large mushrooms, for example, or beneath lots of small, short-lived fruit bodies. These variations in reproduc-tive strategy account for a good deal of the diversity in mushroom form, and additional permutations in the arrangement of the fertile tissues—ripples or spines rather than gills or tubes—encompass fur-ther variety. Natural selection ensures that any particular fruit body form will operate properly: if the spores are not dispersed in sufficient numbers, the genes they carry are destined for elimination.

But adaptation isn't the whole picture: biology is filled with examples in which the adaptive value of particular genetically encoded features are not determined by their enhanced mechani-cal operation. Closely related species of beetle can occur in a range of sizes and with horns of varying elaboration. These differences may have arisen for no other reason than a successful pairing of long-horned midgets whose descendants alienated themselves from their larger short-horned kin, becoming, in time, separate species. This is sexual selection. The same sort of mechanism may help explain why there are so many species of the mushroom genus

Russula: 750 of them, all with white gills, but with caps in every color of the rainbow. None of the obvious guesses about adaptive value provide a satisfying explanation here, so sexual selection may be the answer.

Long before Darwin's insights about evolutionary mechanisms, natural historians sought to carve the living world into groups of organisms with shared characteristics. The common anatomical features of mammals, for example, are evident without any knowledge of their origins; accordingly, Linnaeus assembled them under the Class Mammalia in 1758. In retrospect, this identification of shared physical features worked quite well, allowing Linnaeus to situate *Homo sapiens* beside our primate relatives without invoking doubts about the biblical account of creation. The Linnean practice of arranging species within genera, genera within orders, and orders within classes has survived the molecular genetic analyses of the last quarter century. In fact, many of the eighteenth-century groupings of animals and plants still make sense in light of our contemporary perspective: shared characteristics often reflect shared ancestry. This approach, though, has proven misleading for mycology, and many of the original combinations of fungal species cannot be arranged on a sensible evolutionary tree.

Early systems for classifying fungi relied upon their most conspicuous structural features, separating everything with gills into one group, those with tubes into another, and so on.[4] Christiaan Hendrik Persoon (1761–1836) systematized the fungi using this method during a thirty-year period of feverish scholarship in Paris, during which he lived as a poverty-stricken recluse in a sixth-floor garret (Fig. 3.2a). A competing system of classification was constructed by Elias Magnus Fries (1794–1878), who described thousands of species for the first time and relied on spore colors to differentiate between specific groupings, or series, of mushrooms

(a)   (b)

Figure 3.2. European pioneers of fungal classification. (a) Christiaan Hendrik Persoon (1761–1836). (b) Elias Magnus Fries (1794–1878).
Source: From C. G. Lloyd, *Mycological Notes* (1898–1925).

(Fig. 3.2b). In his early writings, Fries, influenced by German romantic philosophy, posited that four influences, called the *cosmica momenta*, were responsible for generating fungi. The action of a nebulous force, or *nisus reproductivus* (earth and water), would initiate the fruit body, and subsequent interactions with air, heat, and light would situate the resulting creation in one of four classes established by Fries. The Swede adopted a more rational approach to taxonomy in his middle age, but showed little interest in the Darwinian revolution that would, eventually, expose the chaos in his schemes.

Describing mushrooms according to their appearance is a useful activity. These portraits provide the only reliable way to identify anything in the field and to decide, perhaps, whether to eat it. Since Darwin, however, the science of taxonomy has been motivated by the ultimate goal of naming and arranging organisms in *natural* classifications that reflect evolutionary affinities. There is no *a priori* reason to suppose that lumping all gilled mushrooms in one group, then subdividing this into brown-spored and white-spored species, and so on, à la Persoon and Fries, would be a hopeless tactic for achieving this goal, but it is. Pier Andrea Saccardo (1845–1920) thought he had found a better method than Fries by nesting species whose spores looked similar under the microscope.[5] These details proved no better than macroscopic features at reflecting hereditary relationships.

Genetic comparison is the only objective approach to understanding relatedness. The technique has been remarkably successful in beginning the long process of disentangling species previously assigned to the "wrong" groups and carving out new assemblages that represent evolutionary ties. This exercise has revitalized the study of fungal taxonomy for a generation of academics (mostly American) and simultaneously infuriated experts who have witnessed the wholesale dismissal of familiar species' names and groupings. Many of the traditional groupings of mushrooms with shared structural features fall apart at the genetic level. The reason that the classical reliance upon observation led to an erroneous picture of fungal evolution is convergence. Because the common umbrella shape is so effective at dropping spores into the air, the feature has emerged multiple times during the evolution of the basidiomycetes. Mushrooms aren't like flowers, which are reproductive organs that arose once and were subsequently adapted. They are much more like the wings of bats and birds, evolving independently but looking superficially similar and performing the same function.

Though the *in silico* drudgery of analyzing DNA sequences must be mind-numbing (I've never done it, so perhaps I'm wrong), the technology, and its results, are undeniably impressive. Confidence in the trees built from these analyses has grown as the underlying comparisons between species are based upon larger numbers of genes. These trees are referred to as *phylogenetic trees* because the lengths of the branches that link everything together are scaled to the differences in the sequences and, therefore, reflect evolutionary kinship. Ideally, comparisons would be based upon a complete reading of all of the genes, of the entire genome, of each experimental subject. Genomic analysis has already been used with spectacular success in understanding the evolutionary ties between different species of the yeast *Saccharomyces* and for a handful of filamentous fungi.[6] We are probably a few years away from making this a practical method for looking at most of the mushroom-forming fungi. Indeed, 2008 marked the publication of the first genome of a gilled mushroom: *Laccaria bicolor* is one of the thousands of species whose mycelium hooks itself into the roots of forest trees to form an ectomycorrhizal partnership through which nutrients shuttle between fungus and plant.[7] (I'll come back to this species later in this chapter.) In the meantime, phylogenies based on three, four, or five genes have shown some fascinating results when compared alongside the structural characteristics of the sequenced fungi. The species of *Russula* and diverse relatives with all manner of fruit bodies sit in their own taxonomic *order*, distinct from other gilled mushrooms such as *Amanita*; puffballs are gilled mushrooms, kind of, and, despite their superficial resemblance, not at all related to earth-balls, a type of bolete. Who would have guessed? In a few cases, these surprising, counterintuitive results were predicted, in fact, by investigators who looked at structure, but the picture from the molecular evidence is so much richer and has the additional virtue of being more likely to be true. Shared genes are proof of shared ancestry: we can now say with confidence that the false turkey tail, *Stereum ostrea*, is a relation of *Russula*, just as we can say, without any serious probability of error, that Thomas Jefferson was a very close relation of some of Sally Hemings' children.[8] There is grandeur in this view of life.

Aside from prudent concerns about the closure of herbarium collections and the difficulties of finding employment as a classical taxonomist—one who collects and describes—in this molecular age, it may be important to ask why the evolutionary approach is so important. On what basis is this pursuit of a natural taxonomy so noble, and, therefore, why should we be investing so many resources in the molecular phylogenetic study of fungi? The revelation of unexpected affinities between different-looking mushrooms is exciting, but, one might argue, so is naked paragliding. Should mycologists be doing other things? As the Cornell taxonomist and self-professed curmudgeon Richard Korf has said, there is little point sitting in the lab poring over phylogenetic trees when the fungi are disappearing from nature.[9] The same could be said for much of basic biology. We work in our labs, probing questions that appeal to small groups of specialists, while so much of the biosphere is being extinguished. The suggestion of some prominent biologists, including E. O. Wilson, is to get on with identifying species, to document biological diversity as quickly as possible before, in the words of Jim Morrison, "the whole shithouse goes up in flames."[10] If the biosphere is to be flambéed in its own juices, the inventory will, of course, be of no more use than any other human artifact. That said, I concede that current funding decisions should not be predicated on the approaching clatter of apocalyptic hooves. In the end, it all comes down to one's expectation for the future of humanity. In my humble opinion—thank you for asking—the second half of the twenty-first century will belong to Malthus. His nightmare will be lived by the more than 9 billion people who will struggle for existence after my substance has dispersed in the form of quotidian puffs of carbon dioxide. Nine billion hungry apes will not have any choice but to destroy the remaining forests and extinguish much of the splendor of hundreds of millions of years of evolution. Oh well, *c'est la vie,* or, *c'était la vie.* I hope I'm wrong.

One other problem, while we're considering the topic of molecular phylogenetic studies, is the scarcity of studies on the evolutionary imperatives that drove the development of different groups of fungi. At the time of writing, the majority of the sparse practitioners of mycology in the United States are working hard to understand relationships between species but doing little or nothing to understand the underlying meaning of differences in gill and tube arrangement, spore shape and size, and so on. There are, of course, some notably inspired exceptions, with investigators beginning to probe what the genomic data say about multicellularity in fungi.[11] As I am an old-school experimentalist, scientific meetings of mycologists make me feel like a pork pie at a bar mitzvah, as one long-forgotten British comedian (Alexi Sayle perhaps) put it so eloquently. *C'est la vie.*

Another way to think about mushroom diversity is to consider what these fungi accomplish as residents of ecosystems that teem with other, albeit less interesting, forms of life. Fungi are remarkably busy before they sprout mushrooms, fanning out through the soil and making it more porous, imbuing clay clods with life, and dissolving minerals from rocks; rotting wood and decomposing leaf litter; clothing the roots of forest trees and feeding them with essential elements; attacking many of the same tree species as their parasites; furnishing calories for parasitic orchids and all manner of animals; cooperating with some bacteria and killing others; cohabiting with green algae and cyanobacteria in lichens; stunning invertebrates with toxins and digesting their tissues; and, always, cleansing the environment and making life possible for the rest of us. On the negative side, once in a while a mushroom's spores will take root in an unfortunate person's nose or throat and rot them like a fallen tree.

Mushroom colonies are invisible most of the time, and it takes an act of considerable imagination to appreciate the dependence of a forest on their vitality. When a log is rolled over, or some damp leaves are brushed aside, a white web of the hyphal bundles called cords is often uncovered. A handful of soil from beneath the log will smell intensely mushroomy, but it is difficult to leap from sniffing dirt to realizing that the rest of life on earth, especially the more complex organisms, would be inconvenienced (by which I mean dead) without mycelia. Mushroom colonies are marvelous things, functioning as essential agents of decomposition and dispersing nutrients throughout ecosystems. Their efficiency as recyclers is based on a number of attributes. Their invasive growth process is uniquely suited to the exploration and digestion of a three-dimensional food source, such as a recumbent column of beechwood. The growth mechanism is dependent upon the production of different kinds of enzymes, particularly cellulases that chop up the white fibrous components of wood into smaller and smaller strings of sugar molecules, and lignin-modifying oxidases that deconstruct the brown-tinted aromatic molecules that strengthen timber. Cellulose and lignin decomposition afford mushrooms uncontested access to quadrillions of calories in dead wood on the planet's surface. Differing emphasis on the breakdown of these constituents classifies a mushroom as a brown rot or a white rot fungus. The brown rot species remove more cellulose (turning the wood brown), while the white rot fungi fragment the lignin along with some of the cellulose (leaving a pale pulp). It has been suggested that the evolution of the enzymatic facility for decomposing lignin in the Basidiomycota had such a massive effect upon timber removal that it terminated the hyperaccumulation of plant remains and resulting coal formation at the close of the Carboniferous Period![12]

Some wood-rotting mushrooms are saprotrophs, an epithet shared with mushroom species adapted to leaf putrefaction or the decomposition of animal dung. Others are pathogens of trees and shrubs, digesting the tissues of living plants and continuing to do so postmortem.[13] The bright-orange bracket fungus called chicken of the woods (or sulfur shelf), *Laetiporus sulphureus*, is a hardwood pathogen whose fruit bodies form in vertical stacks up the trunks of their hosts. *Laetiporus* is a brown rot mushroom that thrives on the heartwood of oaks and other species but leaves the sapwood alone, enabling the infected tree to remain standing for many years. The birch polypore, *Piptoporus betulinus*, is another brown rot species that specializes in weeding out older trees within stands of birch. Forests in which the fungus is prevalent are filled with dead and dying trees whose erect posture disguises their amazing fragility: a child can fell infected birch branches with a karate chop—a mild stimulant for his self-esteem (providing the tree doesn't land on him afterward). Among other possessions, the Austrian Iceman, Ötzi, carried pieces of birch polypore when he bequeathed his body to archaeology by bleeding to death and being frozen in a glacier for 5,000 years. The reason for his interest in the fungus is unknown. It has been claimed that it has some medicinal value, which is possible, if for no more compelling reason than the fact that the mushroom is less appetizing as a snack food than a handful of corks. Native Americans expressed similar reverence for other species of bracket fungi, including carved fruit bodies in their medicine bundles, hanging them on necklaces and sacred robes, and mixing their ashes with powdered tobacco for chewing, smoking, and snorting.[14]

A third example of a brown rot fungus is the beefsteak fungus, *Fistulina hepatica*, a blubbery bracket whose cut flesh resembles uncooked liver, as reflected in its Latin sobriquet, or richly marbled steak (Plate 7). Adding to their butcher shop personality, the fruit bodies bleed when squeezed. This species attacks oak wood, staining it with reddish-brown bands and rending the timber into crumbly brown cubes. (The dry rot fungi *Serpula lacrymans* and *Meruliporia incrassata* carry out the same kind of wood decay in buildings.) The structure of the *Fistulina* bracket is unique. Like other species, the spore-producing tissues are arranged within tubes beneath the cap, but the tubes of *Fistulina* are separated from one another, hanging down like little bells. Recent studies show that the fungus is more closely related to the gilled mushrooms than to other species with poroid fruit bodies.[15] It is a lovely thing to encounter in the woods, and the tactile joy obtained by gently palpating its white bells with one's fingertips is not to be missed.

The white rot mushrooms are more common than the brown rotters, and their manner of destroying wood is more ecumenical, attacking just about all of the constituent molecules. The hard woody brackets of *Ganoderma*, mentioned in the previous chapter for their enormous spore output, are supported by white rot colonies that wreck beech trees after they have been infected by other fungi. *Phellinus* species introduce themselves into living trees via dead branches but do not tend to fruit until they have spent a few years expanding up and down the stem from the point of infection. Their fruit bodies are hoof-shaped and so hardened that they appear to be formed from the wood and bark tissues of their hosts. *Armillaria* species, including *Armillaria ostoyae* that produces the huge colonies described in Chapter 1, act as white rot fungi, too. Their colonies develop as saprotrophs, digesting fallen wood and the tree stumps left by broad-leaved trees and conifers. *Armillaria* species can also penetrate living trees and spread through the vital cambium tissue beneath the bark and kill their hosts. White-rot activity by *Armillaria* is evident in a different type of infection when the fungus spreads through the tree without destroying its cambium. Another gilled parasite is the oyster mushroom, *Pleurotus ostreatus*, which gains entry via wounds and causes white rot of its host's heartwood. The fruit bodies of the oyster mushroom, graced with gills, are attached to trees by short stems, and they are delicious edibles, whether cultivated or line-caught (dolphin-safe) in the woods.

A number of these pathogenic wood rotters continue to grow on their hosts' tissues after the plant has died. In this part of their life cycle they compete with other saprotrophic mushroom-forming basidiomycetes that specialize in eating plant remains. *Trametes versicolor*, turkey tail, and *Stereum ostrea*, false turkey tail (distinguished by its smooth-bottomed fruit bodies), form fused clusters of thin brackets whose upper surfaces are colored in concentric stripes. Both cause white rot. The basidiomycete saprotrophs also share their food sources with a variety of ascomycete fungi.

Beyond the woods, mushrooms are exceedingly active as decomposers in grassland ecosystems, unless they have been annihilated by the application of nitrogen fertilizer. Nitrogen is often a limited resource for mushrooms, but too much of the element (in the form of nitrates) is a bad thing. While the physiological metaphor may be a little strained, this might be likened to upsetting lawn care professionals (mistreated in print here because they are such devotees of nitrates and mushroom-free turf) by forcing them to precede their customary lunch with a bowl of seabird guano. Enjoyment of their sandwiches following this Dantean repast would be impaired, just as mushroom colonies are perturbed by the profound changes in soil chemistry caused by fertilization. The cellulose and lignin in grasses, particularly their root systems, serve as the dominant food source for healthy mushrooms. Their colonies may solubilize these plant tissues directly, or they may extract some nutritional value from them after they have passed through the guts of earthworms and other subterranean herbivores or after deposition by an aboveground herbivore like a health-conscious camper (or an African buffalo). Like fungal growth in other habitats, expansion from the germinating spore is centrifugal, but this pattern may be sustained for centuries in stable grasslands to produce fairy rings—naturally occurring halos of mushrooms—with diameters of hundreds of meters. A maximum speed of fairy-ring expansion of more than 1 meter per year has been estimated for a pink-spored mushroom called *Lepista sordida* that "spoils" the turf on Japanese golf courses.[16] This is a very nimble fungus whose hyphae must be elongating at about 2 mm per day, considerably faster than fairy-ring fungi in natural grasslands.

Genetic studies show that rings are formed by individual mycelia, but it isn't clear whether they can develop without mating, from unpaired monokaryotic mycelia (see Chapter 1). Fertile dikaryons are certainly easier to spot, because the subterranean shape of the colony is flagged by the rings of mushrooms. The fairy rings of some fungi are visible only when fruiting occurs, whereas persistent patterns of dead grass or more luxuriant grass are characteristic of other grassland mushrooms including *Agaricus*, the puffball genera *Calvatia* and *Lycoperdon*, and *Marasmius oreades*, the mushroom that bears the elitist ("common") name of the fairy ring champignon. (Which is no more fitting than the name "wise [man] ape," *Homo sapiens*, for another species; Linnaeus never witnessed the problem-solving skills of a bonobo.) The bright-green halo of grass at the edge of many rings is produced when the roots absorb nutrients solubilized by the active mushroom colony and the fungus also releases chemicals that promote plant growth.[17] A zone of exhausted grass may also be created within the same ring where the traveling fungus has depleted the soil. Distinctions between ring types are not very clear and a fungus may kill the overlying grass for a while and then fertilize it in response to rainfall.

It isn't at all surprising that evanescent rings of mushrooms have inspired folktales involving dancing fairies and witches, elves and evil spirits, spells, poisons, and buried treasure. In some parts of England, it was believed that young women could improve their complexion by sprinkling themselves with dew from the richest fairy ring grass, or make a love potion from it if they knew the recipe.[18] Other mushrooms have been similarly employed, the most exotic practice developing in the Ozarks in the nineteenth century, where it was claimed that girls touching their pudenda with the slimy head of a fresh stinkhorn would be lucky in love.[19] I wonder how many girls tested the doctrine of signatures in this fashion? Rings of dead grass led to stories about dragons scorching the ground and to slightly less fanciful writings linking fairy rings to lightning strikes. Lightning improves soil nutrition by catalyzing nitrate formation, but these compounds are flushed from the atmosphere by rain and do not concentrate at the point of electrical contact with the earth. But lightning strikes might promote fruiting via some other process, at least according to the Japanese researchers who are using high-voltage bursts of electricity to stimulate crops of edible mushrooms.[20]

The reality of fairy rings is no less magical than their mythology. When a chunk of turf is chopped from the colony and planted outside or inside its ring, the fungus keeps extending in the original direction with little sideways spread. The graft behaves as if it were still part of the ring. If the sod is turned around in the opposite direction and returned to its hole, the disoriented piece of colony shuts down and dies, leaving a gap. These beautiful experiments demonstrate a number of interesting things. The survival of the turf transplanted from the active part of the ring to the interior shows that the usual absence of growth inside the ring has nothing to do with nutrient depletion. The fairy ring removes a lot of nutrients from the soil as it expands, but these will be replenished by new growth of grass in subsequent years. Nor is the ring leaving toxins in its abandoned center. The direction of growth of the grafts offers proof that the billions of filamentous cells within a fairy ring have a fixed polarity and are programmed to keep doing what they are doing—forging outward—and never growing backward into the older interior portion of the ring.[21] This lack of flexibility on the part of the hyphae contrasts with the spontaneity of the cells in a mushroom (see Chapter 1). The reason for this is a mystery, but it may have something to do with the nutritional interdependence of cells throughout the colony. For the fairy ring, there is no growing back.

Some of the common genera of grassland fungi found in Europe have woodland counterparts elsewhere in the world. Species of waxcap, *Hygrocybe*, for example, produce fairy rings in meadows but also thrive in forests. This overlap in habitat preference among a group of closely related species may be explained by the forested ancestry of most European grassland. This observation supports the idea that there are few fundamental differences between the ways in which woodland and meadow mushrooms operate: they all eat the same kinds of things. It is a bit simplistic to think of mushrooms as vegetarians, however, because they also digest animals.

Lacking much empathy for a tree infected by a bracket fungus, or turfgrass marred by fairy rings (except for golfers), people have a tendency to view the fungi as one of the more sluggish parts of nature—harmless unless we are foolish enough to eat the toxic ones. For all of their beauty, though, mushrooms, like every other living thing, are engaged in a perpetual battle for survival and possess an impressive array of conventional and chemical arms. A medieval weapon called the "morning star" resembled a mace, but with a head decorated by metal spikes. This subtle piece of equipment was used to spoil people's afternoons by whacking it into their faces. Mushrooms use a microscopic morning star to rip open the flesh of nematodes (roundworms), permitting toxins to wash over their glistening viscera. If the nematode is a pregnant mother, then her unborn worms spill through the wound and are terminated by the toxin. The lawyer's wig, *Coprinus comatus*, supplements its diet through this mechanism, colonizing and digesting the injured worms. Other mushrooms attack worms with different devices. These include bulbous and hourglass-shaped adhesive cells that release a nematode-specific superglue (from which the invertebrates can escape only by tearing their outermost layer of "skin") and clusters of spiky cells called acanthocytes that work like the morning stars of *Coprinus*. Chemical weapons are also widespread: the oyster mushroom, *Pleurotus ostreatus*, celebrated earlier for its parasitism of trees, and a common lawn mushroom, *Conocybe lactea*, stun nematodes with toxins produced by secretory cells. In some cases, the mushroom colonies do not follow up by digesting the worms, suggesting that these mechanisms are defensive strategies to prevent the worms from feeding on the hyphae.

Mushrooms rarely eat live vertebrates, though a distant single-celled relative called *Cryptococcus neoformans* is one of the better-known opportunistic fungal pathogens of humans. Having said this, unfortunately, there are some unpleasant case histories of *homnivorous* mushrooms that deserve a brief mention. *Schizophyllum commune*, a little stick-dwelling white mushroom whose gills are divided up their middles, shows up from time to time as an infection of the nasal or sphenoid sinuses of otherwise healthy patients. Colonies of the mushroom have also been identified in lung infections, brain abscesses, and ulcers on the roof of the mouth. In some of the infections, the initial symptoms of mushroom attack were as modest as a sensation of nasal obstruction. Another mushroom that dines on human flesh is *Inonotus tropicalis*, a white-rot fungus that usually entertains itself by making poroid brackets. This species was detected in an aspirate from a patient's bone marrow, and its hyphae filled an abscess next to the person's spine. Other bracket fungi have caused lung infections, and *Coprinopsis cinerea*, an ink cap, has outdone them all, colonizing a prosthetic heart valve.

For every instance of an infection or poisoning caused by a mushroom (toxicity is the subject of Chapter 7), there are innumerable examples of relationships between fungi and other forms of life that benefit two or more participants. These are called mutualistic symbioses, or mutualisms, for short. The gilled mushroom *Leucoagaricus* (also known as *Leucocoprinus*) *gongylophorus* is a mutualist, protected and fed by leaf-cutter ants in underground nests populated by millions of insects.[22] The biggest nests contain hundreds of football-sized fungus gardens connected by tunnels. Most of the ants are sterile female workers that chew off pieces of leaf, carry them to the gardens, and feed them to their fungal partner. What is the benefit to the ants? The fungus is highly efficient at digesting nutrients within the leaves—something the ant cannot do on its own—and converts a high proportion of the calories into nourishing hyphal branches, fattened structures called gongylidia or bromatia, that serve as the ant's staple. This symbiosis can be seen throughout the warmer parts of South and Central America, north into Mexico and the southeastern United States, and in the Caribbean.

Each nest is founded by a young queen that imports the fungus on her nuptial flight. Once established, the mushroom colony is fed a continuous supply of leaf fragments by different castes of worker ants. Workers also remove the spores of other fungi so theirs grow unmolested. In addition to the physical removal of foreign spores, the ants carry a bacterium on their cuticles that produces an antibiotic. This antibiotic targets a parasitic fungus called *Escovopsis* (an ascomycete) that would otherwise destroy the gardens, but the farmed mushroom is immune to the substance. Additional chemicals are released from a structure called the metapleural gland on the ant thorax. These control other microbes on the ant surface without removing the bacterium that controls the *Escovopsis*. The workers are skilled at removing fruit-body primordia to avoid the diversion of energy from the manufacture of gongylidia, which sustains the colony. This is the reason that the fungus produces mushrooms and disperses its spores from abandoned nests. The relationship between the mushrooms and the leaf-cutter ants is thought to have evolved relatively recently, between 5 and 15 million years ago, from less sophisticated unions between gardener ants that cultivate their fungi on a more varied diet of insect excrement and body parts, and fragments of rotting wood.

In Africa and elsewhere in the Old World, mushrooms in the genus *Termitomyces* are cultivated by termites within mounds of dried mud.[23] The termites eat dead plant materials and fabricate a framework for their fungus gardens, called a comb, from their cellulose-rich feces. Cellulose decomposition in the gardens is optimized within the large cathedral-shaped mounds that keep the colony ventilated through a warren of air channels.[24] Recent research suggests that the fungi in some mounds assume a great deal of responsibility for their own livelihood, by forming a dry surface around the wet comb interior that prevents the growth of other kinds of fungi. When the insects abandon the nest, the West African species *Termitomyces titanicus* produces an enormous mushroom with a cap diameter of 1 meter.[25] The mutualism evolved in the African rainforests, but termite colonies supported by fungus gardens have since become more important ecologically in open savanna habitats, where they represent a major source of carbon dioxide emissions. Fungus-growing termites are important crop pests in some regions, which is also true of the leaf-cutter ants in South America.

Ants and termites are the best-known symbionts with mushrooms, but there are plenty of other examples. The larvae of beetles form burrows in wood digested by fungi, with the fungus manured by the insect and the beetle eating the pre-pulped wood. Many insects feed on the tissues of fruit bodies and distribute spores, stinkhorns offering an obvious example, but shake any mushroom and insects engaged in obscure relationships will drop from the gills. Subterranean relatives of mushrooms called false truffles are also dispersed by animals, but in their case, squirrels and other small mammals unearth their fruit bodies, attracted by unidentified perfumes to the cache of oil-rich spores. *Rhizopogon* is a widespread false truffle genus that is closely related to the bolete genus *Suillus*.

Most lichens are mutualisms involving ascomycete fungi, but a few are formed between mushrooms and photosynthetic algae or cyanobacteria. Until recently, it was thought that these basidiolichens were restricted to the tropics, but their known distribution has expanded in light of more recent surveys. Nevertheless, the basidiolichens are not viewed as particularly important symbioses by anyone other than basidiolichen experts. It is, of course, futile to try to rank symbioses in order of their ecological significance. (Ecological significance is like biological success: I have no idea what either term means.) Ecologists, who should have a clearer concept of these things, did their best to ignore fungi for a very long time but have embraced mycorrhizal mutualisms between mushrooms and plants with great enthusiasm in recent decades. This interest in mycorrhizae has spread among other biologists, too, and the existence of these mutualisms is one of the few reasons that fungi garner any pages in introductory textbooks. While this limited attention to the fungi is disgraceful, at least student appreciation of symbiosis has at last been pushed beyond the sea anemone and its bloody clownfish![26]

There are almost 8,000 species of mushrooms that form mycorrhizae: that's half of all of the mushroom-forming Basidiomycota.

The actual number may exceed 20,000 species, because we have identified only a sliver of the world's mushrooms and other fungi. There are many types of fungal association with roots, but the ecto-mycorrhiza is the predominant manifestation of this in the mushrooms.[27] As the name suggests, the fungus is visible on the outside of the root. The association is initiated by the mycelium attaching to the root of a tree or woody shrub. Encountering a fringe of root hairs in the soil, the fungus senses that a potential partner is close by and alters its growth pattern, enveloping the hairs and ramifying over the cylindrical root surface. More hyphae are recruited to the root and these cells branch repeatedly, forming a tight-fitting glove called the mantle. Cascades of chemical signals pass between plant and fungus as they resolve whether to accept or reject one another. The root continues to extend, and the fungus keeps pace by elongating its own hyphae. As the mantle thickens, the normal pattern of cell division within the root system is disrupted, and its finest branches are transformed into fattened and stubby structures referred to as short roots. Meanwhile, the mushroom colony penetrates the root surface, sending exploratory hyphae through the walls between individual plant cells. These cells use their internal turgor pressure to force their way between the strands of cell wall material and probably release enzymes to ease their passage.

As the symbiosis deepens, this intercellular growth can become so elaborate that the normal connections between root cells are replaced by uninterrupted barriers of fungal cells. This internal part of the mycorrhiza is known as a Hartig net, after Theodor Hartig, a German botanist who described the structure in the 1840s (Fig. 3.3). Struck by the unusual anatomy of the mycorrhizal root, he thought that the net was an innate part of the plant rather than a fungal associate. In this position, the fungus gains complete control over the transfer of nutrients between the outermost cells of the root and begins

Figure 3.3. Mycorrhizal root showing exterior mantle of the ectomycorrhizal fungus and hyphae growing between the host epidermal cells to form the Hartig net. *Source:* Adapted from H. B. Massicotte et al., *Canadian Journal of Botany* 64, 177–192 (1986), with permission.

to absorb a substantial proportion of the sugars formed by the plant. If the relationship between fungus and plant was defined solely by this flow of sugars, we would characterize it as parasitic, but the plant benefits from the partnership, too. Beyond the mantle, the fungal mycelium spreads through the soil, creating a network of filamentous hyphae that act as a gigantic sponge, funneling water and dissolved elements toward the plant. The fungal colony operates as an accessory root system, allowing the plant to access water and dissolved elements, particularly phosphorus, from an enormous volume of soil. Estimates suggest that 1,000 meters of hyphae may explore the soil for every meter of root. In nutrient-poor alkaline soils, this is a lifesaver for the tree, offsetting the sugar payment to the fungus. Colonies of some ectomycorrhizal mushrooms are even capable of etching passages in solid rock, participating in the slow dissolution of granite under shallow soils and shuttling leached elements to the roots of their partners.

The fact that the processes necessary for living in harmony with a tree have arisen repeatedly among the mushrooms, and that the same anatomy develops every time, suggests that the evolutionary journey from saprotroph to symbiont is less complicated than we might have assumed. Rather than arguing for an astonishingly unlikely degree of convergence, the manifestation of a mantle and Hartig net in these associations is, probably, an inevitable consequence of the physical intimacy required for shipping nutrients between a root and the filamentous colony of a mushroom. In other words, when the hyphae of a fungus penetrate the walls of the root cells, they are always going to splurge sideways to form the kind of pavement of cells that is recognizable in the Hartig net. This shape results from the mechanical interaction between fungus and plant. Indeed, hyphae have the same squashed appearance in root infections caused by pathogenic fungi, the difference being that the pathogen will often migrate into the root cells themselves and digest their contents if it can evade the plant's defenses. Much of the difference in outcome between a mycorrhizal symbiosis and a disease is due to the different molecular "conversations" between the fungus and its host. Signaling mechanisms are at the heart of these relationships.

Laccaria bicolor is a pretty species that forms mycorrhizae with pine, fir, birch, and poplar trees (Plate 8). Its bronze cap can expand to a diameter of 7 centimeters and supports striking lilac gills as a youngster. Like other *Laccaria* species, it suffers from the pejorative common name of "deceiver," which refers to the way that the bright colors of these mushrooms fade as they get older, rendering them difficult to identify. It has a wide distribution, growing in association with trees throughout the temperate and boreal forests. Besides its mycorrhizal nature and geographical spread, *Laccaria bicolor* was chosen for sequencing because it is amenable to experimentation in the lab. It is also important in tree nurseries, where it is added to soil to boost seedling growth. Its genome is quite large, some 65 million base pairs (As and Ts, Gs and Cs), but is dwarfed by the 3 billion or so rungs on the ladder of the human genome.[28] When we look at the number of genes that encode proteins the comparison is more humbling: 20,000 for the mushroom; between 20,000 and 25,000 for us.[29] This reflects the astonishing amount of junk DNA in the human genome that doesn't correspond to any proteins. In other words, a mushroom's genome is a lot more streamlined than an ape's.

Laccaria bicolor produces hundreds of enzymes that degrade proteins, fats, and carbohydrates in the soil, but it lacks the usual catalysts for decomposing the cellulose and lignin of plant cell walls found in other mushrooms. This is significant, because it seems likely that *Laccaria* and other mycorrhizal fungi evolved from wood-rotting ancestors and must have lost these enzymes as they adopted their new lifestyle. For comparison, the genome of a white rot fungus called *Phanaerochaete chrysosporium* encodes 100 separate enzymes for oxidizing lignin.[30] The inventory of protein-degrading enzymes in *Laccaria* is interesting in light of the discovery that the mushroom is a predator of springtails, paralyzing these little soil arthropods with a toxin and then digesting them with its hyphae.[31] Springtail corpses provide a rich source of nitrogen, and the transfer of a portion of this harvest to the tree is further incentive for the plant to maintain the symbiosis. The *Laccaria* genome also encodes hundreds of small proteins that are released from its hyphae when it is partnered with tree roots. This is the Hartig net's song to its tree: "Everything is OK.... I'm not here to kill you.... Thanks for the sugar and here's some phosphorus and nitrogen.... Everything is still OK...."

Only 3% or so of all seed plants form ectomycorrhizal associations, but the ecological and commercial importance of the symbiosis is incalculable. Trees in the conifer family, the Pinaceae, and the flowering plants of the Fagaceae are all mycorrhizal.[32] This means that the conifers of the northern boreal forests are mycorrhizal, along with the dominant, broad-leaved trees of the temperate forests and vast swaths of Southeast Asia. In recent years, mycologists have also begun to appreciate the importance of the mycorrhizal symbiosis in the wet tropics, and mushrooms are known to hook up with the roots of the rainforest trees in the dipterocarp and legume families. Through their relationships with these trees, mushrooms are essential for timber production, climate control and atmospheric chemistry, water purification, and the maintenance of global biodiversity. In more parochial terms, there would be no *us* without them— humans evolved in ecosystems dependent upon mushrooms, and we would perish without their continual activity.

Ancestors of mushrooms evolved long before any of the plant groups with which they establish mycorrhizae today. This suggests that different kinds of saprotrophic species may have jettisoned their taste for decomposing prehistoric plant tissues in favor of the sugars offered by the living roots of newly evolved plants. Associations with conifer roots, for example, may have originated with the diversification of the pine family in the Cretaceous, or, even earlier, in the Permian. Ectomycorrhizae with flowering plants are a more recent invention—their proliferation has been linked to the period of global cooling ushered in at the close of the Eocene, when temperate forests blossomed across the northern hemisphere. Genetic evidence also suggests that tube-bearing mushrooms related to today's *Boletus* and *Suillus* diversified in the Eocene, furnishing a fresh slate of partners for plants open to the possibility of a merger.

Individual plants can form active mycorrhizae with ten or more fungal species, and in different regions a single plant species can form mycorrhizae with thousands of kinds of fungi. With tree species like the Scotch pine, *Pinus sylvestris*, flourishing over enormous transcontinental ranges, the advantage of mycorrhizal flexibility is obvious: plants can work with the native fungi wherever their seeds germinate. Some fungi are flexible too, though others show greater discretion. So whereas promiscuous *Russula* species will inveigle their way into the roots of almost anything dressed in bark, a kind of slippery jack, *Suillus pungens*, shows utter fidelity to two types of pine endemic to coastal forests in northern California.

Mushrooms form different kinds of mycorrhizal relationships with parasitic plants, including orchids.[33] All orchids produce minuscule seeds and are dependent upon cohabitation with a fungal colony for germination and early development. Most orchids dispense with this infant dependency once they grow up, because they turn green and can make their own food.[34] Chlorophyll-lacking parasitic orchids, including the bird's-nest orchid *Neottia nidus-avis*, rely upon the fungi throughout their lives. This relationship is different from the ectomycorrhizal symbiosis, because these ghostly, achlorophyllous plants live by digesting the coils of fungal hyphae called peletons in their roots. They are mycoheterotrophs: parasites on mushrooms. There is a third player in this relationship: the same mushrooms form mycorrhizae with green plants, channeling food from the roots of a photosynthetic tree to their blanched orchid symbionts. *Russula* species are common participants in these tripartite associations, and some individual orchids partner with multiple fungal species at the same time. Other kinds of plants engage in the same relationships with mushrooms, including members of the gentian family, and *Monotropa uniflora*, known variously as the ghost plant, Indian pipe, and corpse plant.

Mycorrhizal mushrooms are among the favorite edible fungi collected by mycophagists, human and otherwise, all over the world. Through this passive function in global ecology as a food source for animals, mushrooms exert their most familiar roles in civilization. Having introduced the biology of the mushrooms in the first three chapters, I'll turn next to this subject of sociomycology: the uses and misuses of mushrooms. The whole history of our species can be told through our interactions with mushrooms, from our continuing emancipation from superstition to our forthcoming demise. "Consider the lily," the Bible recommends; "consider the mushroom" opens a richer vein.

Chapter 4

Satan's Gourmand

HARVESTING WILD MUSHROOMS

Mount Gretna, Pennsylvania. October 1898. The gentlest rain was spitting in the wood fire; the sun setting behind the spindly maple trees. Charles McIlvaine removed his cap, wiped his forehead with a rag, and, leaning toward the fire, stirred the suspended iron pot. "What in Sam Hill are you brewing in there, Captain?" said his companion, returning to the camp with an armful of logs. "Pennypacker, you are about to join me in a supper fit for saints," announced McIlvaine.

"Vittles for sinners more likely, Old Ironguts. I'll settle my stomach with the salt pork. Pass the whiskey."

McIlvaine removed his ladle from the pot, blowing on it to cool the stew, and took a sip. "Would you guess that an unbirthed pecker could taste so good, Colonel?" he asked, and he passed the ladle to his companion. In the clear broth floated warmed slices of stinkhorn eggs, each consisting of a chocolate-brown paste held in a thin gelatinous casing. "Maybe they're better fried, but what do you think?"

Pennypacker nibbled at a slice and spit the pellet into the fire. "You are a goddamned madman, Captain! I'd rather eat bear scat."

Charles McIlvaine and Galusha Pennypacker became friends during the Civil War, when they served together in the 97th Regiment, Pennsylvania Volunteer Infantry. McIlvaine headed a company called the Greble Guards, and Pennypacker was a senior officer in the regiment. The former was honorably discharged in 1863. Two years later, Pennypacker was shot through his right hip during an assault on Fort Fischer, on Cape Fear River in North Carolina; he was not expected to survive.[1] After the war, McIlvaine found it difficult to settle into a profession, so he roamed Europe, eventually returning to America to live in the mountains of West Virginia. In the Appalachian wilderness, he had an epiphany:

> While riding on horseback through the dense forests of that great unfenced state, I saw on every side luxuriant growths of fungi, so inviting in color, cleanliness and flesh that it occurred to me they ought to be eaten.... Up to this time I had been living, literally, on the fat of the land—bacon; but my studies enabled me to supplement this, the staple dish of the state, with a vegetable luxury that centuries ago graced the dinners of the Caesars. So absorbing did the study become from gastronomic, culinary and scientific points of view, that I have continued it ever since, with thorough intellectual enjoyment and much gratification of appetite as my reward.[2]

The conversation above must have been a familiar one for McIlvaine, though he was never one to be deterred by another's palate. The intrepid eater sampled almost every fungal thing he found in the woods—rejections were rare. In his classic work, *One Thousand American Fungi*, the old soldier described the delicious, the bland, the unpleasant, the repellent, and the toxic. Of the oyster mushroom, *Pleurotus ostreatus*, McIlvaine wrote, "The camel is gratefully called the ship of the desert; the oyster mushroom is the shellfish of the forest. When tender parts are dipped in egg, rolled in bread crumbs, and fried as an oyster they are not excelled by any vegetable, and are worthy of place in the daintiest menu." *Boletus piperatus* obtained a less enthusiastic endorsement: "It has been eaten by the writer and his friends with enjoyment *and* without any discomfort." (The italicization is mine; would you visit a restaurant whose review concluded, "Overall, I enjoyed the eclectic menu and neither my wife, nor myself, experienced any violent evacuation whatsoever"?) *Tricholoma coryphaeum* is damned with similarly faint praise: "All disagreeable odor…disappears upon cooking." *Polyporus heteroclitus*, a bracket fungus, is best picked young because, "As it ages it becomes offensive." Conversely, *Amanitopsis nivalis* has a bitterness that "appears to develop while cooking." Worse still was *Tricholoma sulphureum*: "No amount of cooking removes its unpleasant flavor. I have tried to eat enough of it to test its qualities, but was satisfied after strenuous efforts to mark it INEDIBLE." Yet McIlvaine was impressively tolerant of other species listed as TOXIC in today's guidebooks, including Satan's bolete, *Boletus satanus*, and its relative, *Boletus luridus*. One last example defies simple categorization based on palatability, or lack thereof. The jelly fungus, *Syzygospora mycetophila,* forms little parasitic lozenges on mushroom caps: "Separating them was taking the host from the parasite." (I'm licking my lips already.) "Cooked it is glutinous, tender—like calf's head. Rather tasteless." McIlvaine, in other words, was Satan's gourmand.

One Thousand American Fungi was a tremendous work of scholarship. As late as 1898, two years before its publication, McIlvaine planned to stop at 500 species, but the manuscript kept growing.[3] To increase coverage within a single printed volume, he was forced to cut 50,000 words from his descriptions. The resulting 700-page, richly illustrated, family-Bible-sized tome remains in print after more than a century, and McIlvaine is rightly celebrated as a hero of amateur mycology (Fig. 4.1).[4] (I use "amateur" here, not as a pejorative term, but to distinguish people who love collecting, identifying, and

Figure 4.1. Captain Charles McIlvaine (1840–1909) and one of his previously unpublished portraits of an unidentified mushroom.
Source: McIlvaine photograph reproduced from cover of *McIlvainea* 1 (1972).

eating mushrooms from the merry band of mycologists who toil in the academy.) In addition to his reflexive delight in the diversity of mushrooms in West Virginia, McIlvaine became fascinated by an article titled "Toadstool-eating" that appeared in *The Popular Science Monthly* in 1877.[5] The author, Julius Palmer, went on to publish *Mushrooms of America: Edible and Poisonous* in 1885,[6] a progenitor of McIlvaine's great work that was nonetheless unacknowledged by Old Ironguts. Both authors saw the potential of wild mushrooms as a free food source and understood the importance of identifying the toxic ones. McIlvaine and Palmer shared this avocation with professional scientists, including Thomas Taylor, a microscopist at the U.S. Department of Agriculture (USDA), and Charles Horton Peck, New York State botanist. Another notable figure in this nineteenth-century pursuit was Berry Benson, a former sharpshooter and scout for the Confederate army who rivaled McIlvaine in his degustatory experiments. Benson ate the fly agaric, *Amanita muscaria,* often celebrated for its psychoactive properties, "increasing the quantity every break-fast...till I was surfeited."[7] He reported no ill effects, other than mentioning in his correspondence with Peck that the mushroom once made him feel "a little light-headed."

Amateur mycology is thriving today in the United States. Local and state mushroom societies are affiliated with a national organization, the North American Mycological Association (NAMA), which was established fifty years ago by an Ohioan, Harry Knighton. The identification, collection, and consumption of wild mushrooms are major activities for NAMA, bringing me, in a roundabout way, to the subject of wild mushroom collecting and conservation in the twenty-first century.

As my appreciation of mushrooms has increased, I've developed an aversion to seeing them spread on tables—dehydrating, shriveling, and stanched from releasing spores—before being transferred to the trash, where they disintegrate into a stinking mush. A familiar sight at the end of weekend forays organized by local associations of mushroom enthusiasts, the aim of this extravagant autopsy is to exhibit the diversity of the day's finds and to help participants learn the art and science of identification. My reaction is a personal one, a sensitivity to the objects of my scientific obsession, rather than an immediate concern about damaging the populations of fungi from which the mushrooms were picked. (This is little different, I suppose, from my distaste at seeing snails squashed on sidewalks, or unfortunate turtles on highways, confused by the traffic.) I'm not looking for psychoanalysis here, but the more I think about this, the less confident I become in the validity of "truths" about mushroom collecting promulgated by established mycologists. Roy Watling, a well-known British expert, suggests, "Picking mushrooms does not generally create a threat to the species as replacement fruit bodies are already in place under the surface and ready to grow. The removal of the dominant fruit body by picking will stimulate their growth, provided the weather conditions remain favourable."[8] Is this true? Are mushrooms like wild blackberries, fruits that can be picked to exhaustion without ever harming the plant? The answer to these questions by the majority of mycologists and supported by all of the available experimentation is, surprisingly, "Yes."

One of the best studies on the picking question was conducted in Switzerland.[9] The researchers looked at two sites, beginning in the 1970s in an old-growth forest and then extending the work to a 110-year-old plantation of Norway spruce. The investigators surrounded a series of plots with fences to keep out mushroom pickers and then picked or trampled some plots themselves, subjected others to picking *and* trampling, and designated additional plots for protection from both activities. Every edible mushroom was removed from the picked plots. Trampling was avoided by the use of catwalks. They also studied the effects of harvesting by pulling the fruit bodies from the ground versus cutting their throats (severing their stipes) with a knife. Over a period of thirty years, the Swiss study revealed no changes in the diversity of edible mushroom species, nor in the number of fruit bodies of each species, in the picked compared with the nonpicked plots. But trampling was highly disruptive to the fungi, causing a 30–40% decrease in the number of fruit bodies.

The interpretation of these results requires some subtle analysis. You might infer from the trampling effect that the delicate mycelium of the mushrooms was crushed to death by the collective hooves of grossly overweight Swiss researchers. Similar studies of chanterelles in Oregon show that although the effects of trampling are severe, they may be short-lived: fruiting patterns recovered after a year without human traffic. One possibility is that trampling squishes the primordia of the mushrooms (Watling's "replacement fruit-bodies") without harming the larger colony. So, the studies are in, and we should get out and harvest all of the edible mushrooms that we can find, feeling confident that we are incapable of harming the supporting colonies.

Not so fast, Professor Moriarty! We have a record of ignoring the precarious state of species until it is too late. My thinking about mushrooms is likely influenced by my fascination with the biological holocaust perpetrated in the Midwest in the nineteenth century. I have often imagined how the skies above our farmlands must have once looked, clouded by millions of passenger pigeons. A Select Committee reporting to the Ohio Senate in 1857 affirmed, "The Passenger Pigeon needs no protection. Wonderfully prolific, having the vast forests of the North as its breeding grounds, traveling hundreds of miles in search of food, it is here to-day and elsewhere to-morrow, and no ordinary destruction can lessen them, or be missed from the myriads that are yearly produced."[10] Children who learned to hunt the birds in the 1850s would, in their dotage, witness the pigeons' extinction. Mushrooms have a rather different breeding strategy from pigeons, but they are not exempt from the indispensable link between reproduction and one's genes having an opportunity to enjoy themselves in the future. No eggs, no pigeons; no spores, no mushrooms.

The part mushrooms play in reproducing the species from which they are formed is complicated. Mushroom colonies certainly mate according to the description in Chapter 1, and the spores are released in amazing numbers, as I explained in Chapter 2. Mushrooms are the reproductive organs of basidiomycete fungi, but the effect of destroying them isn't as obvious as the experimental sterilization of every male Javan rhinoceros—I picked this species because there are very few of them left—using a set of very sharp scissors and an excellent pair of running shoes. In the mammalian example, the rhinos would vanish within a few years of the pruning. Even consistently plucked of every mushroom, every year, though, large wild colonies of some species of fungi might persist—though the odds are against this in the long term. The active portion of the colony might run out of food, or the environment might change for the worse in some other way, or the colony might be struck by an aggressive fungus or soil predator. Mushroom sex and spore release are the natural buffers against these challenges: fusion of colonies of different mating types introduces variation into mushroom populations, and new colonies originate from spores. Without mating and spore release, genetic diversity withers, and inbred species become vulnerable to the exigencies of environmental change. The health of the Swiss plots subjected to three decades of picking might have been maintained by the intrusion of spores from the unpicked plots or from older colonies that grew into them. So, while a handful of careful studies on the effects of mushroom picking indicate no problem with the removal of mushrooms, they may be missing the effects of the kind of intensive harvesting that is taking place in many parts of the world.

Mushroom picking is big business in the Pacific Northwest, with colossal harvests of chanterelles (*Cantharellus* species), boletes, and matsutake (*Tricholoma magnivelare*). These species are illustrated in Plate 9. The scalloped fruit bodies of morels (*Morchella* species) are also worth a fortune, and I mention them here even though they are ascomycetes rather than basidiomycetes. The exact tonnage of fruit bodies taken from these forests is not known, because the harvest is unregulated over vast areas. Data gathered from Oregon, Washington, and Idaho in the 1990s estimated that annual hauls peaked at 2,000 metric tons, valued at $41 million.[11] Over much of the region, wild mushrooms rank far lower in value than the trees with which they are associated.[12] The relative value of the forest commodities changes in favor of the mushrooms when we look at the places where the American matsutake prospers—individual fruit bodies of this fungus can command more than $200 when sold in Japan.[13] Japanese chefs cook matsutake in a variety of ways—adding the fragrant fruit bodies to *sukiyaki* and frying them to make crispy *tempura* are two popular methods—and as domestic harvests of the matsutake have fallen 100-fold in the last 50 years, American imports have skyrocketed in value.[14] This means that in the matsutake forests, the mushrooms are at least as valuable as the timber. Having said all of this, it is important to remember that the essential symbioses between mushrooms and trees means that neither partner can exist in isolation.

Today's McIlvainites have little effect on this rural economy. Amateur mycologists pick for their kitchens or simply for the fun of the hunt. The serious mushroom harvesting is done by casual laborers, the term belying the back-breaking task of picking mushrooms from sunup to sundown. Mushroom picking is regulated via the distribution of permits, and purchasing these is a big part of the valuation of the fungi versus the trees discussed above. In the Northwest, the pickers come from all ethnic groups but share the fate of chronic underemployment beyond the forests. The activity of pickers from immigrant communities, including Hmong, Mien, and Lao from Southeast Asia, is often highlighted in news stories about mushroom harvesting. Their participation in the autumn harvest adds to the exotic nature of the business, perhaps, but plenty of poor white and Hispanic Americans spend the fall mushroom season in the woods as well. The involvement of these economically marginalized pickers is one of the reasons why the issue of mushroom harvesting has become politicized. This may also explain why questions about the sustainability of commercial picking are met with animosity, or, more often, ignored.[15]

David Arora, author of *Mushrooms Demystified*,[16] one of the most popular guides to mushroom identification, is a strong advocate for the rights of pickers and highly critical of efforts to regulate the harvest. He contrasts the policies in the western United States with the "everyman's right" approach to picking in Canada and Scandinavia.[17] One sympathetic commentator views the implementation of surveillance policies aimed at regulating pickers as a form of "disciplinary power" by "the nation-state forest management regime" that seeks to coerce people "to behave in desired ways of their own volition."[18] The same might be said about highway speed limits. Those opposed to the regulation of mushroom picking make some logical points when they stick to the facts of the research, but I disagree with their assessment of human behavior and the ability of local populations to manage resources for themselves. Rhinoceroses, Javan or otherwise (with or without their genitals—it's their horns that are prized by poachers), would soon be gone without restrictions on poachers.

With or without regulation, wild American mushrooms likely have a rosier future than their relatives in Asia. China is the global leader in harvesting wild mushrooms, with a decade-old estimate of 308,000 tons for the domestic and export market.[19] The 2,000-ton combined crop from Washington, Oregon, and Idaho is less than 1% of this mountain of Chinese mushrooms. This must be considered in relation to the fact that China has half the forest cover of the United States: the Chinese are engaged in the planet's definitive experiment on the effects of intensive mushroom picking.

The Asian species of matsutake, *Tricholoma matsutake*, is the most valuable mushroom in China and is harvested in the mountainous province of Yunnan. In a 2008 article, Arora described a visit to the province and his amazement at seeing magnificent houses in villages that he had assumed would be among the poorest in the region.[20] Summer harvesting of matsutake was responsible for the economic boom. The mushrooms are sold several times by middle-men (though Arora found that most of these entrepreneurs were middlewomen) before they leave the local markets and are exported to Japan. More than 1,000 tons of matsutake are dispatched from China in a productive year, dwarfing the American harvest.[21] With livelihoods at stake, it is not surprising that there are conflicts between villages over access to the best forest sites. Disagreements have resulted in long-running legal battles, property damage, and, in at least one case, murder.[22] Disputes among pickers are not limited to Asia, however—advocates of everyman's rights might imagine that arguments about mushrooms can be settled over a cup of cof-fee, but the idea that American pickers are peaceful hippies who practice free love with their fellow woodspeople is a fairy tale.[23] Pickers get very upset when they feel that their harvests are being "stolen" from "their" mushroom patches. A potential complication with American pickers is that, unlike their Chinese comrades, they have a right to bear arms. All of this favors, in my opinion, some regulation of picking, even if the effects upon the mushrooms them-selves prove benign.

There is, as you might have imagined, more to mushroom picking than matsutake. Chanterelles are a valuable crop in North America and Europe, and porcini, *Boletus edulis*, is big business in Italy and is also harvested in Eastern Europe, China, and southern Africa. Porcini is exported from the Pacific Northwest as well. Mushrooms that are important in local markets include the termite-associated species of *Termitomyces*, sold in Africa and India, and the milk cap, *Lactarius deliciosus*, a favorite in Eastern Europe. Captain McIlvaine would have been gratified to have learned that his own affection for the phallic mushroom was dignified a century later by the sale of its dried fruit bodies in China.[24] In addition to morels, trade in other wild ascomycetes includes false morels, *Gyromitra* species, the caterpillar parasite, *Cordyceps sinensis*, and—the most expensive of all edible fungi—truffles.[25] *Cordyceps*, reaped with horrifying intensity in the Himalayas, and European truffles eclipse the combined value of all of the basidiomycete mushrooms. While the life cycles of some of these ascomycetes are quite different from the behavior of the basidiomycetes, the conservation issues are similar. No spores, no mushrooms.

Mushroom species differ in their sensitivity to picking. A mycorrhizal species that cohabits with one or two types of tree in a handful of counties in California, for example, is more vulnerable than the cosmopolitan chanterelle. Mushrooms that decompose tree stumps might be more resilient than mycorrhizal boletes, but a saprotroph that is limited to decomposing the wood of a single kind of tree is surely as susceptible to extinction as its mycorrhizal relative. Visions of mycorrhizal sensitivity and saprotrophic fragility may be illusions. Morels that fruit in great numbers after forest fires are probably safer than specialized tree parasites, but we don't have any experimental data to verify these guesses. More important than trampling and picking are threats to mushrooms from the interrelated effects of habitat destruction, atmospheric pollution, and climate change. A commentary in *Science* bore the provocative title, "Disappearing Mushrooms: Another Mass Extinction?" This suggests that these global problems pose an unprecedented threat to the survival of mycorrhizal fungi and their trees.[26] Recognition of these challenges, rather than concerns about picking, are the usual justification for adding mushrooms to national red lists of endangered species. Bulgaria, for example, red lists a total of 215 mushrooms (including ascomycetes) and 37 of these are considered critically endangered.[27] A more cautious assessment of threatened fungi throughout Europe, authored by Swedish researchers, considers 33 species. These include gilled and poroid mushrooms and brackets, a stalked puffball called *Tulostoma niveum*, and *Gomphus clavatus*, which looks like a short, fat chanterelle.[28] Given its global purview, the International Union for Conservation of Nature and Natural Resources (IUCN) is cautious to the point of absurdity, listing only one fungus as a threatened species, a gourmet mushroom from Sicily called *Pleurotus nebrodensis*.[29] Ironically, the rarity of the mushroom has stimulated greater picking and is pushing the species toward extinction. Sicilians must really love their mushrooms and, at the risk of waking up next to a horse's head (again), I surmise that their lobbyists at the IUCN make offers that are not open to discussion.

Picking mushrooms as a hobby is quite different from doing it for a living. The scale of mushrooming for personal consumption varies widely according to local availability, of course, and upon the degree of cultural acceptance of wild foods. The Russians and the British offer a study in contrasts. Mushrooming is celebrated in Russian literature, and people in rural areas remain some of the most passionate mycophiles on the planet. The British are traditional mycophobics, but the diversification of their culinary tastes in recent decades has greatly stimulated the market for domestic and imported mushrooms. The "discovery" of wild mushrooms by the British brings with it obvious hazards and has caused some spectacular poisonings (Chapter 7). In his sixteenth-century *Herball*, herbalist John Gerard warned, "one maner is deedly and sleeth them that eateth of them and be called tode stoles."[30] "Mushroom" was reserved for edible fruit bodies in Gerard's scheme. The term was also adopted in a more restrictive sense for a single species: the field mushroom, *Agaricus campestris*. The basis for this colloquialism was probably that the field mushroom was the only species most British people learned to pick and eat without worrying about being poisoned. Returning to Gerard's sense of the words, the distinction seems pointless once we realize that the edible fruit body of the field mushroom can look very similar to a noxious relative called the yellow stainer, *Agaricus xanthodermus*. "These white fruit bodies look alike, but the one that bruises yellow is a toadstool and the one that doesn't is a mushroom," is an example of correct, but essentially useless, usage.[31]

The first edition of Gerard's *Herball* was published in 1597, joining only a handful of earlier illustrated works on fungi that considered their edibility, including books by the renaissance botanists Pietro Andrea Mattioli, Mathias de l'Obel, and Giambattista della Porta. Mattioli and later writers drew much of their inspiration from the works of the Greek physician and botanist, Pedanius Dioscorides, and his Roman contemporary, Pliny. Drawing on the superstitions of his era, Pliny believed that the breath of serpents was responsible for making mushrooms noxious and cautioned people to avoid fungi that grew close to serpent's dens. These delusory associations between venomous animals and mushrooms persisted for two millennia, and, amazingly, continue to hold some sway in modern mythology (Chapter 6).

Jules-Charles l'Éscluse, Latinized as Carolus Clusius, was one of the first investigators to offer a sensible view of the fungi. In the 1570s, he served as a botanist at the behest of the Viennese court of Emperor Maximillian II and collected mushrooms in Central Europe. On these excursions, he was accompanied by a priest and a watercolorist. Scholars believe that the painter was Esaya le Gillon, Clusius' nephew, and his paintings of fungi in their natural settings became known as the *Clusius Codex*.[32] Following Maximillian's death, Clusius fell from the grace of the Viennese court and was eventually appointed a professor at the University of Leiden. In

Holland, he prepared his magnum opus, a panoptic study of botany titled *Rariorum Plantarum Historia*. The mushroom illustrations in this work were supposed to have been based on the *Codex*, but they were mislaid by the publisher, and new woodcuts of mushrooms were substituted. Clusius is best known for establishing the botanical gardens in Leiden, called the *Hortus Botanicus*, and for his work on tulip "breaking"—the mixing of coloration due to a virus—that helped stimulate the speculation in tulips that climaxed, after his death, in the tulipomania of the 1630s.[33] But his *Codex* wasn't lost forever. (Cue alarming music, clouds racing across a blackening sky, and cut to Tom Hanks standing in a fairy ring and raising an eyebrow to portray immense cleverness: *The Clusius Code*.)

Sixty years after Clusius was buried, Professor Robert Langdon, no, sorry, Franciscus van Sterbeeck rediscovered the *Clusius Codex*. A Flemish priest and a member of the nobility in Antwerp, Sterbeeck was slowed by chronic illness in attending to his priestly duties and afforded an opportunity to pursue his interest in botany. When Sterbeeck was shown the paintings by a botanical colleague in 1672, his response was along the lines of, "Mother of God, these are beautiful. I'm going to use these in my great work on fungi because I have the artistic skills of a flatworm." This might not be a perfect translation from the Flemish, but this is exactly what Sterbeeck proceeded to do. More than half of the unattributed illustrations in his *Theatrum Fungorum*, published in 1675, were printed from copperplate engravings transcribed directly from the *Codex* (Plate 10).[34] Additional illustrations of fungi came from another work by Clusius and still more from other Renaissance botanists.

The practice of copying illustrations was widespread in the seventeenth century, but Sterbeeck went further than others, claiming that most of his figures were based on direct observation from nature.[35] His plagiarism seems to have escaped detection, however, because the *Codex* disappeared again for 200 years. It reappeared in the library of the University of Leiden in the nineteenth century (and remains there today). Regardless of the source of the illustrations, Sterbeeck's book was the first serious attempt to demystify mushrooms. Under the influence of a growing community of Italian merchants living in Antwerp, Flemish readers of *Theatrum Fungorum* were beginning to embrace the use of wild mushrooms in their cookery. Sterbeeck wrote for the common folk, guiding them in their identification of the poisonous and the delectable and introducing them to the medicinal uses of fungi. But if the *Clusius Codex* hadn't disappeared for 200 years, it is unlikely that historians would have expended so much ink on Sterbeeck's contributions to mycology.[36]

Sterbeeck's work was also predated by another collection of fabulous mycological illustrations. This one was commissioned in the 1620s by Federico Cesi, Prince of Acquasparta, a town in central Italy. Cesi, who founded the Accademia dei Lincei, believed that study of fungal growth and reproduction held the promise of elucidating some of the fundamental mysteries of life. Galileo became a member of the Lincei and aided its studies on fungi with the gift of a new instrument for which the academy's secretary, Giovanni Faber, invented the name "microscope." Like the work of Clusius, the *Cesi Codex* was thought to have been lost forever. In this case, Napoleon's army swiped Cesi's drawings from their Italian owners in the eighteenth century. Two centuries later, they were rediscovered in Paris by an Italian scholar, Andrea Ubrizy Savoia.[37]

As I discussed in Chapter 1, the real genius of mycology, the first investigator to carry out experiments on fungi, was Micheli. Micheli's *Nova Plantarum Genera* was never designed as a field guide, but an experienced mushroomer can identify many species from the descriptions and extraordinary illustrations.[38] The task is complicated greatly by the fact that Micheli was working a full century before Linnaeus and so included no binomials in the book. The stinkhorn, *Phallus impudicus*, is described as "Phallus vulgaris, tortus albus, volva rotunda, pilcolo cellulato, ac fumma parte mbiloco pervio, ornato," which, according to my erudite colleague Mike Vincent, means: "the common Phallus, with a white body, a rounded shell, and an ornate chambered cap that proceeds to a navel at the tip." Where Linnaeus gave us genus and species, Micheli fused the name of the organism with its distinguishing features. *Nova Plantarum Genera* was never lost, but Micheli's research was forgotten anyway, and the study of mushrooms languished for another century. Lists of species, or regional mushroom "floras," were compiled by the early American mycologists, including two clergymen, Lewis David de Schweinitz and Moses Ashley Curtis.[39] Schweinitz died in 1834, and his collection of "Exotic Fungi" was studied by Curtis, who collaborated with the British clergyman mycologist Miles Berkeley. Berkeley's knowledge of fungal diversity was unmatched in his era, but he became famous for experiments that identified the microbial cause of the potato famine. His discovery was a scientific triumph fought over the superstitions of many fellow devotees of Christ who believed that the potato famine was God's "gift" to the Irish people. Through his potato-famine work, Berkeley became a major figure in the rebirth of experimental mycology, a field that was otherwise dominated by Heinrich Anton de Bary and his German peers, in the middle of the nineteenth century (Chapter 1). Berkeley was also an honorary member of the Woolhope Field Naturalists' Club, an extraordinary organization that may have invented the "sport" of the mushroom foray in the 1860s.[40] Here is an excerpt from a newspaper article describing their activities:

> The Woolhope Naturalists' Field Club, one of the oldest and largest of the local societies established for the practical study of natural history, has its headquarters at Hereford, and is especially

distinguished for the attention it pays to the mysteries of mycology and mycophagy. Every autumn its members meet together for what is termed "A Foray among the Funguses," and the enthusiasm displayed on these occasions is apt to excite no little amusement in the district where the search is carried on.[41]

The article also described the club dinners after the forays and shared the members' wisdom about cooking mushrooms:

Almost all agarics, it must be remembered, are rather rich, and should therefore be eaten in moderation. To eat them as accompaniments to meat is an obvious error; they should form a separate course, and Burgundy will be found the most suitable wine to drink with them.

As a recent recruit to pescetarianism, I'll leave you to figure out whether to eat mushrooms with or without mammal flesh, but I affirm the soundness of pairing mushrooms with the finest wines available to humanity. The forays organized by the Woolhope and continued by the Yorkshire Naturalists' Union served as the inspiration for the foundation of the British Mycological Society in 1896—the organization has more than 2,000 members today. Its counterpart, the Mycological Society of America, was founded in 1932. Both societies are dedicated to promoting research on fungi but are rooted in the collection and identification of mushrooms.

Today's mushroomers have many reasons for enjoying their hobby: learning and exercising the craft of identification and collecting for the kitchen are the most popular reasons for mushrooming, in addition to the collateral benefits to one's physical and mental health from spending time in the woods rather than *in silico*.[42] Club members do love their mushroom autopsies, and many well-meaning aficionados seem to revel in posing with huge mush-rooms for their friends and for the camera, even the inedible ones. "Folk artists" express no shame in chiseling a fifty-year-old bracket from a tree and turning it into an etching of woodland creatures. Why do people view mushrooms as so different from other liv-ing things? A mushrooming magazine is open next to me, featur-ing a photograph of a middle-aged woman proffering an enormous bolete that she has loosened from the ground. The cap is as big as her head. She is grinning as if she won the lottery and evincing almost unsustainable joy. Why did she detach this beautiful fruit body from its colony and its moisture source? Mushrooms are never going to attract the same kind of reverence as polar bears and other charismatic megafauna—I'm resigned to this—but such beautifully constructed things merit more than the ignominy of festering into slime in a trash can. Imagine a meeting of a local Audubon Society that ended with the janitor tossing a sack of songbird eggs into the dumpster.

Plate 1. Blood-foot, *Mycena haematopus*, showing beads of bloody sap clinging •
to the stipe (stem) surface.
Source: From J. E. Lange, *Flora Agaricina Danica*, vol. 2 (Copenhagen: Recato, 1936).

Plate 2. *Calvatia gigantea*, the giant puffball.
Source: Painting by John Augustus Knapp, courtesy of Lloyd Library and Museum,
Cincinnati.

Plate 3. *Hygrocybe conica*, the witch's hat. The stem of this mushroom becomes blackened when bruised. Many guidebooks list this as poisonous, but adventurous mycologists continue to debate its edibility.

Source: Painting by John Augustus Knapp, courtesy of Lloyd Library and Museum, Cincinnati.

Plate 4. Diversity of fruit-body form in the Russulales. (a) Gilled mushroom *Russula lepida*. (b) Hydnoid or toothed fruit body of *Auriscalpium vulgare* growing from pine cone. (c) Flattened fruit body of *Stereum ostrea*, the false turkey tail.

Source: (a) From J. E. Lange, *Flora Agaricina Danica*, vol. 5 (Copenhagen: Recato, 1940). (b) From P. Bulliard, *Histoire des Champignons de la France* (Paris: Chez L'auteur, Barrois, Belin, Croullebois, Bazan, 1791). (c) From G. Inzenga, *Funghi Siciliani Studii*, vol. 2 (Palermo: Di Francesco Lao, 1869).

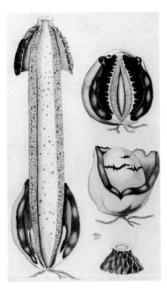

Plate 5. *Phallus impudicus*, the stinkhorn; mature fruit body and egg stage.
Source: From R. K. Greville, *Scottish Cryptogamic Flora*, vol. 4 (Edinburgh: Maclachlan and Stewart, 1826).

Plate 6. *Amanita muscaria*, the fly agaric, and *Hygrocybe conica*, witch's cap.
Source: From M. C. Cooke, *Edible and Poisonous Fungi: What to Eat and What to Avoid* (London: Society for Promoting Christian Knowledge, 1894).

Plate 7. The beefsteak fungus, *Fistulina hepatica*, whose spores are released from tubular bells (detail top right) that hang from the underside of the fleshy fruit body.

Source: From W. H. Gibson, *Our Edible Toadstools and Mushrooms and How to Distinguish Them* (Harper & Brothers, 1895).

Plate 8. *Laccaria bicolor*, whose genome was sequenced in 2008.

Source: Photograph courtesy of Lawrence Livermore National Laboratory, Livermore, California.

Plate 9. Prized edible mushrooms. (a) *Cantharellus cibarius*, chanterelles. (b) *Tricholoma magnivelare*, matsutake. (c) *Boletus edulis*, king boletes or ceps.
Source: (a) Painting by John Augustus Knapp, courtesy of Lloyd Library and Museum, Cincinnati. (b) From S. Kawamura, *Illustrations of Japanese Fungi* (Tokyo: The Bureau of Forestry, 1911–1925). (c) From A. Venturi, *I Miceti dell' Agro Bresciano* (Brescia: Dalla Tipografia Gilberti, 1863)

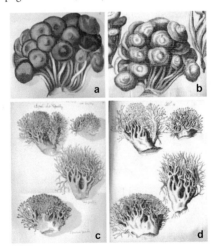

Plate 10. Examples of Sterbeeck's use of the *Clusius Codex* in his *Theatrum Fungorum*.
Source: (a) and (c) are *Codex* watercolors from Gyula Istvánffi, *Etudes et Commentaires sur le Code de l'Éscluse*; (b) and (d) are from Franciscus van Sterbeeck, *Theatrum Fungorum*.

Plate 11. *Agaricus campestris*, the meadow mushroom.
Source: Painting by John Augustus Knapp, courtesy of Lloyd Library and Museum, Cincinnati.

Plate 12. *Tricholoma equestre*.
Source: From J. E. Lange, *Flora Agaricina Danica*, vol. 1 (Copenhagen: Recato, 1935).

Plate 13. *Cortinarius speciosissimus*, a deadly web cap. Compare with chanterelles shown in Plate 9a, with which this poisonous species has been mistaken. *Source:* From M. C. Cooke, *Illustrations of British Fungi (Hymenomycetes)*, vol. 4 (London: Williams and Norgate, 1884–1886), in which the fungus was called *Cortinarius rubellus*.

Plate 14. *Amanita phalloides*, the death cap.
Source: From R. D. de la Rivière, *Le Poison des Amanites Mortelles* (Paris: Masson, 1933).

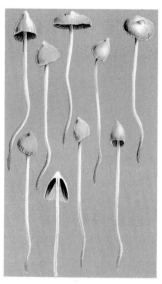

Plate 15. *Psilocybe semilanceata*, liberty caps. The common name refers to the limp, conical caps, called Phrygian caps, that became a symbol of liberty for French revolutionaries in the eighteenth century.
Source: From M. C. Cooke, *Illustrations of British Fungi* (*Hymenomycetes*), vol. 4 (London: Williams and Norgate, 1884–1886).

Plate 16. Giant fruit body of *Ganoderma tsugae*, a close relative of *Ganoderma lucidum*, reishi, spending quality time with the author in Ohio.

Chapter 5

Snow White and Baby Bella

THE GLOBAL INDUSTRY OF
MUSHROOM CULTIVATION

The technician clicks "Start," interrupting the darkness of the chilly shed with spots of light emanating from slender beams that play over the compost beds on the sunken floor. Each light beam shines from the end of a robotic arm that glides along a gantry of rails slung from the ceiling. The room is a flurry of activity, with arms reaching onto the beds, suctioning the caps of white mushrooms to their rubber cups, lifting the fruit bodies from their compost, rotating, and dropping them onto conveyor belts running beside the beds. With labor accounting for almost half the cost of mushroom production, the entire cultivation process is ripe for automation. This is one of the reasons that researchers in the United Kingdom have been developing robot pickers. They need electricity, lots of it, and lubrication, but they don't get paid, don't take lunch breaks, and never complain. A nonunionized staff of six robots could pick 2 million mushrooms in a week, equivalent to the harvest by thirty poorly paid, bored, and exhausted humans.[1]

The practice of cultivating mushrooms on animal dung was invented in France during the reign of Louis XIV, and has changed little in 300 years. Few people aspire to the monotony and exhaustion of working with millions of white things sticking out of manure-filled beds, of course, but financial exigencies push people to handle mushrooms in preference to all manner of other more objectionable things (Belgian sex tourists spring to mind). An English clergyman, the Reverend William Hanbury, wrote about mushroom growing in his treatise on gardening published in 1770:

> The practice of raising mushrooms in gardens is now becoming general among gardeners of eminence; and though such mushrooms are very much inferior to those gathered from pastures, yet there is this great advantage attending the practice, that they may be obtained at unusual times, or when they are not to be met with in the common fields.[2]

Reflecting the confusion about the reproductive process of mushrooms in the eighteenth century, Hanbury described the deposition of the seeds beneath the fruit bodies and formation of primordia in the soil. His method of cultivation relied upon the careful unearthing of clusters of primordia from natural mushroom colonies. This precious "spawn" was used to fertilize beds of fermenting horse dung mixed with straw. People on both sides of the English Channel may have been doing much the same for centuries before Hanbury's description, but his codification of the method was a part of the larger revolution in British agricultural practices driven by a burgeoning population and facilitated by tremendous advances in mechanization. "Mill-track" spawn, obtained from the manure deposited by horses shackled to mill wheels, gained a strong reputation for its productivity, but growers prized any "virgin" source. This was considered vastly superior to spawn that was transferred from one bed to another, though this method took some of the guesswork out of the process and ensured that the correct species was raised. The correct species, *the* mushroom, was *Agaricus campestris* (Plate 11). The Anglo-French love affair with this fungus is interesting in light of the Roman abhorrence of the field mushroom. Official market inspectors purportedly ruled that baskets of this mushroom, called *pratiolo*, and no others, be thrown into the Tiber.[3]

The mushroom-growing process was transferred underground by Parisians in the nineteenth century. Serpentine beds of manure were mounded in disused stone quarries that became known as *champignonières*, or mushroom caves (Fig. 5.1). Almost 2,000 kilometers of mushroom beds were under cultivation beneath the Parisian suburbs before the First World War.[4] In the United States, Quaker farmers experimented with mushroom cultivation in Pennsylvania. William Swayne was the most successful of these entrepreneurs. A florist, he grew mushrooms beneath greenhouse benches, enclosing the space with burlap to gain better control over temperature and humidity. Impressed with the results, Swayne gave up growing flowers and built a mushroom house in Kennett Square, which allowed him to optimize the climate for his mushrooms. Many sources suggest that Swayne built the first mushroom house, but British and

Figure 5.1. Nineteenth-century mushroom cave beneath a Parisian suburb.
Source: From W. Robinson, *Mushroom Culture: Its Extension and Improvement* (London: Frederick Warne, 1870).

Russian designs for similar buildings are described in magazine articles in the 1870s.[5] Irrespective of national claims to the invention of
the mushroom house, the American mushroom industry flourished
in eastern Pennsylvania, where growers were continually supplied
with horse dung from Philadelphia.

A significant advance in mushroom cultivation occurred in
the 1890s, when French scientists patented a method for making
spawn from spores, affording better prospects for quality control
by selecting particular strains for their productivity and flavor. This
"flake spawn" was first produced at the Pasteur Institute and then
commercialized, allowing the French to dominate mushroom production for many years. A competing product, "brick spawn," was
widely used in Britain, where growers worked in mushroom houses
and—on a much smaller scale—in caves and abandoned railway
tunnels. Brick spawn was made by inoculating compressed rectan-
guloids of compost with virgin spawn.

In the United States, imported spawn obtained a dreadful reputation, because it was ruined either during its lengthy shipment
or due to improper storage upon arrival. Basic research at the U.S.
Department of Agriculture (USDA) Bureau of Plant Industry led
to a new method for making spawn in 1905, providing domestic
competition. The limitations of transferring spawn from one compost heap to the next are obvious to growers. As long as the mycelium is kept well fed with fermenting manure, it seems logical that
the fungus will grow and produce fruit bodies. This isn't the case.
There seems to be an aging phenomenon that bears comparison
to the gustatory and sexual appetites of lotharios on cruise ships:
even with limitless access to the onboard buffet, everyone goes
flaccid in the end. The same natural rule—the Law of Diminishing
Erections—that "everything runs out of steam eventually" plays
out in the laboratory when we transplant, or sub-culture, fungal

colonies from one agar-filled Petri dish to the next. Each time this process is repeated, the colonies spread across the fresh gelified surface, but sooner or later the transplanted fungus tires and its hyphae elongate more slowly than they did in their youth. Often, the colonies stop producing spores. Mushroom growers and lab researchers have never figured out how to mimic nature properly for the fungi they imprison. The USDA came close by making use of the fact that mushrooms are made from stem cells. These cells are capable of producing new colonies if they are extracted from the fruit body and placed on nutrient medium (Chapter 1).[6] Spawn grown from this interior mushroom tissue works better than spawn transferred from mushroom bed to mushroom bed. The reason for the effectiveness of this unnatural process is not known, but it might relate to the unusually free-spirited nature of the cells inside mushrooms. They are the fungal equivalents of the vibrant and developmentally uncommitted stem cells in our bone marrow.

The French method circumvented the serial transfer problem by generating fresh spawn from spores. This seems ideal, because it offers the closest match to the natural life cycle of *Agaricus campestris* in which a mushroom-producing colony develops from airborne spores landing on a manure-rich pasture. But the USDA method had the immediate effect of allowing American mushroom growers to meet the needs of the domestic market without importing European spawn. The French were furious. Nonetheless, the American mushroom crop increased greatly after the introduction of the new method of spawn production. Pennsylvania continued to lead the country in cultivating the fruit bodies, accounting for 85% of mushroom production in the United States in the 1930s.

In her classic 1872 cookbook, *Common Sense in the Household*, Marion Harland wrote of mushrooms, "Have nothing to do with them until you are an excellent judge between the true and false."[7]

After including an alarmingly vague guide to identifying *Agaricus campestris*, though, she goes on to recommend their consumption with recipes for stewed mushrooms, baked mushrooms, broiled mushrooms, mushroom sauce ("pour over boiled chickens, rabbits, etc."), and mushroom catsup. Mushroom catsup, a forerunner of tomato ketchup, was a common condiment in the nineteenth century. Harland's recipe called for steeping mushrooms in brine for three days before boiling them with ginger, mace, and cayenne for five hours. You can try making mushroom catsup for yourself, or taste a facsimile containing "mushroom powder" (powdered mushrooms, I suppose), in the form of *George Watkins Mushroom Ketchup*, manufactured in Britain since 1830. British companies exported mushroom catsup to the United States, competing with domestic varieties sold by H. J. Heinz Company—based in Pittsburgh—and other manufacturers. Canned mushrooms became exceedingly popular in the twentieth century, and the American market was saturated with imports from Europe and Asia, where growers benefited from cheaper labor costs. Pennsylvania growers survived by meeting the demand for fresh mushrooms and a steady increase in mushroom consumption was the result of successful marketing by the American Mushroom Institute, formed in the 1950s.

Global production of *Agaricus* exceeds 2 million tons, dominated by a Chinese harvest in excess of 600,000 tons.[8] The United States is the second largest grower, approaching 400,000 tons of mushrooms (outweighing a supertanker) valued at close to $1 billion. Most of the American crop is picked by low-wage workers employed by 112 domestic growers, and more than half of the production is based in a single county—Chester County—in Pennsylvania.[9] France is now the fourth biggest grower, and the United Kingdom is ninth, just behind Ireland. But none of this megatonnage includes fruit bodies of the meadow mushroom, *Agaricus campestris*. The original "mushroom" is still picked by aficionados for personal consumption, but these fruit bodies are absent from grocery stores today. Growers from Beijing to Kennett Square harvest its domesticated relative, a fungus called *Agaricus bisporus*. What happened?

The source of the original collection, or collections, of *Agaricus bisporus* is not known, though it was somewhere in Western Europe. The universal adoption of this species suggests that its advantages over the meadow mushroom must have been conspicuous. Superior taste may have been an early attribute—a curious decision in light of the blandness of its descendants today. Another asset may have been resistance to disease in the original stock, plus reduced spore production, possibly softening the misery of mushroom picking for workers sensitive to airborne allergens. Unlike the meadow mushroom, *Agaricus bisporus* produces a pair of spores from each of the basidia that project from its gills (Chapter 2). Most other mushrooms form four spores per basidium and package one nucleus in each; *Agaricus bisporus* produces two spores and stuffs two nuclei in each. This seeming trifle of cell biology has major consequences after the spores are released and germinate. Normally, a young mushroom colony contains millions of identical copies of the single nucleus carried by its founding spore. As I have already described, a new generation of mushrooms forms only after a pair of compatible colonies mate. *Agaricus bisporus* can bypass this step, because the colonies that form when its spores germinate are already equipped with a compatible mixture of two types of nuclei.[10] Each spore carries the full complement of instructions for producing a new generation of mushrooms and spores. This means that the qualities of the daughter mushrooms are assured. Beautiful white button mushrooms will produce beautiful white button mushrooms. No need for any messy business with an alien sexual partner: perfect virgin birth follows perfect virgin birth down the great river of time.

The abolition of sex during the evolution of *Agaricus bisporus* might seem advantageous for an agricultural product. The majority of fruits and vegetables are grown as clones of their parents, which is why bananas always taste the same. This kind of quality control is associated with the inevitable burdens of inbreeding, including susceptibility to annihilation through epidemic disease.[11] A farrago of plagues afflict this strenuously inbred crop: *Agaricus* fruit bodies are attacked by fungi that cause diseases, including wet and dry bubble, brown spot, *Trichoderma* spot or blotch, cobweb, mat disease, green mold, and plaster mold. Other fungi spoil the mushroom beds by invading them like weeds; bacteria cause blotching and pitting of mushroom caps, and the curse of drippy gill disease, and inbred mushrooms are also destroyed by viruses, nematode worms, and insects. Once in a while, however, a variant mushroom explores the air above its bed of compost. This mutant may have blotchy skin, may have a wrinkled cap, or may split along its rim. Or it may be whiter than any other mushroom in history, free from the slightest blemish, its pale rind stretched as taut as the skin over a Botox-injected forehead. A mushroom with these latter characteristics discovered in the 1920s was named Snow White.[12] Before Snow White, all of the cultivated strains of *Agaricus bisporus* were brownish or cream-colored. Snow White changed everything. She was the French Golden Delicious of the mushroom industry, her quadrillions of offspring offering shoppers a reliable supply of unblemished, albeit rather tasteless, buttons.

Mushroom breeders have made considerable efforts to develop hybrid strains of the mushroom with improved characteristics. The unusual life cycle of the button mushroom is a tremendous hindrance to this work, but there have been a few successes. One of the techniques breeders use is to isolate infertile spores, which are spores that carry a single nucleus rather than the usual pair. Colonies derived from these spores can then be mated and, if originating from different parent strains, may yield a new variety with useful features. This was the method used to produce two hybrid strains in the Netherlands, designated Horst® U1 and Horst® U3, which are grown all over the world today.[13]

When a bed of *Agaricus bisporus* is allowed to produce a series of flushes of mushrooms, the second or third crops will form fruit bodies with big brown caps and brown gills if they are not picked in the button stage. Of no interest to grocery stores, these fruit bodies were taken home by pickers until clever marketing popularized these elderly mushrooms as a novel flavor for salads, vehicle for varied stuffings, and vegetarian substitute for a hamburger patty.[14] The big brown caps were named portabella mushrooms (also spelled portobello) and are a triumph for the mushroom industry, akin to repackaging tap water in plastic bottles as a low-calorie fashion statement. The success of portabella mushrooms in the last decade has led to much greater interest in brownish varieties of *Agaricus bisporus*. Crimini mushrooms, also known as baby bellas, are another version of the portabella, picked early, before their caps expand very much. Buttons, portabellas, and crimini mushrooms are the same species. The fact that portabella and crimini were born without any fundamental changes in growing practice or genetic innovation adds to the brilliance of this commercial achievement. This was about the only way to reinvigorate the basic product, since the mushroom is so fixated on self-fertility and uninterested in betterment through outbreeding.

The lack of global variability among commercial strains means that any novel characteristics are unlikely to be uncovered through traditional breeding efforts. Genetic prospecting in nature offers an alternative approach. Wild populations of *Agaricus bisporus* have been studied in North America and Europe.[15] These fungi may be mycorrhizal, because each population fruits under specific kinds of trees and shrubs: under native confers in Monterey, California, mesquite in the Sonoran Desert, and spruce in Alberta. The wild genomes of these fungi have the potential to invigorate their cultivated cousins using molecular genetics to transform the strains that have been shackled to compost for decades. A community of researchers is studying the genome of the cultivated mushroom and one of its wild Californian relatives. Beyond commercial growers, investigators working on biofuel production are interested in this genome research and, in particular, the efficiency with which this fungus transforms solid waste into plump mushrooms. This seems like an important research venture to me; after all, there are few examples of biochemical virtuosity that eclipse the transformation of manure into pizza topping.

Like every other agricultural practice, mushroom growing is an attempt to enhance a natural process. Despite my empathy for mushrooms, I'm not going to suggest that there is anything abusive about raising mushrooms indoors, only that the buttons grown in sheds are as far from nature as factory-farmed pigs fattened in colossal barns. Today's method of cultivation does not differ radically from the original technique used in Parisian caves, but it is more reliable, and the yields are considerably better. Recipes for mushroom compost vary from country to country and from grower to grower, but wheat or rice straw and some kind of manure usually constitute the bulk of the mixture, to which corncobs and other plant materials are often added, and supplements include gypsum, lime, and brewery residues. This compost is arranged in piles and allowed to cook for a couple of weeks through the heating activity of thermophilic bacteria. The internal temperature of the compost heap can reach 80°C. In the second phase of the process, the material is spread out over wooden pallets in steam rooms. Steaming the compost is a pasteurization measure that kills nematode worms, insects, and other pests. This procedure leaves some microbes intact, and these play an essential role in removing ammonia from the compost before it is inoculated with mushroom spawn. Careful manipulation of temperature, relative humidity, and carbon dioxide in the growing rooms is important throughout the growing process. The moisture content of the compost is also critical. Many of these environmental variables are controlled by computers in modern mushroom farms. After twelve to twenty days of colony development, a thin layer of peat and limestone is spread over the compost. This "casing" stimulates mushroom formation in about three weeks, and up to three crops, or "flushes," are picked before the entire process is repeated. I have omitted many details from this description but have outlined the basic elements of the method.[16]

Agaricus bisporus was the only mushroom sold in American grocery stores for most of the twentieth century, and growers were often frustrated by the difficulty in convincing shoppers that this most innocuous species was safe to eat. The marketplace today looks very different, with a variety of cultivated mushrooms reflecting the broadening tastes of consumers. Shiitake, *Lentinula edodes*, is the second best-selling mushroom, with 90% of the production occurring in China. Thousand-year-old records from the Song Dynasty describe cultivating shiitake on logs, and the wild mushroom was consumed long before this. Shiitake is the "black mushroom" in Chinese cuisine, and it is one of the multiple ingredients in the vegetarian delicacy known as Buddha's delight. Chinese physicians also associated shiitake with all kinds of health benefits, and modern claims about the power of this unassuming wood-decay mushroom to combat cancer and heart disease, slow aging, and give 60-year-old sun worshipers the complexion of teenage models have made a lot of money for a lot of people (about whom I'll say more in the last chapter). Fourteenth-century Chinese cultivation methods refer to *Lentinula* as the "nice-smelling mushroom"; shiitake is a more recent Japanese name, referring to the source of the logs—the *shii* tree, *Castanopsis cuspidata* in the beech family—on which the mushroom is grown. According to ancient practice, trees were felled, clefts were cut into the logs with an axe, the logs were covered with soil for one year, then watered and beaten with a wooden club. After a spell of warm weather, the mushrooms emerged from the contused logs. Log cultivation is the primary method used today, with plugs of spawn pressed into holes "like tamping tobacco into a pipe," removing the uncertainty of fungal growth attending the classical Chinese practice.[17] The logs are then stacked upright in a "laying yard" for six months or more, before being soaking with water. Beating with clubs is no longer part of the recommended process. The mushroom is also raised from plastic bags filled with sawdust and various additives.

Other popular cultivated mushrooms are also wood-rotting saprotrophs that fruit on logs. These include the winter mushroom or enokitake, *Flammulina velutipes*, and the oyster mushroom, *Pleurotus ostreatus*. The latter produces a fleshy bracket, an enormous spore-shedder that has caused a lot of suffering for pickers.[18] Workers who inhale the spores can develop extrinsic allergic alveolitis, a type of respiratory illness with a distinctive immunological signature. Symptoms include fever, chills, coughing, and shortness of breath within a few hours of exposure, and more serious respiratory complications can develop after prolonged inhalation of spores. People who work with other species can also suffer from this condition, referred to as "mushroom worker's lung," but button mushrooms cause fewer problems because they are harvested before their caps open and spore release begins. Lung problems in the mushroom industry have stimulated interest in mutant oyster mushrooms in which spore formation is blocked, in the hope that these may be used to develop a hypoallergenic commercial strain. Even in the absence of spores, mushroom workers are plagued by other illnesses during every stage of the growing process. The thermophilic bacteria that flourish in the compost before the spawn is added represent one of these allergenic hazards. The specific name for this entry into the encyclopedia of ailments in the mushroom industry is mushroom compost worker's lung. This isn't a problem, of course, for species like the oyster, which are grown on logs.

Almost all of the global crop of millions of tons of cultivated mushrooms are gilled. Exceptions include the wood ear, *Auricularia auricula* (and relatives), and the silver ear, *Tremella fuciformis*. The wood ear forms rubbery, brownish fruit bodies that shed spores from their lower surface. Very popular in Asian cuisine, it is cultivated on logs like the oyster mushroom. Most of the harvest is sold dried; the fruit bodies rapidly expand when they are steeped in warm water. The silver ear is grown on sawdust and forms white translucent sponges of leaf-like folds that are dried and sold in big plastic packages. Other cultivated mushrooms that shed their spores from structures other than gills include a toothy growth called the monkey-head mushroom (lion's mane in North America), *Hericium erinaceus*; maitake or dancing mushroom (also hen-of-the-woods), *Grifola frondosa*; a stinkhorn, *Phallus indusiatus*; and the important medicinal mushroom called reishi, *Ganoderma lucidum*, that is grown from wood buried in soil.

A survey of all of the cultivated species reveals a number of interesting features. If we look at their evolutionary relationships, we find that these species are scattered all over the phylogenetic tree. The button mushroom, shiitake, winter mushroom, and oyster all come from the same taxonomic order, the Agaricales, but sit in distantly related families. The wood ear, lion's mane, hen-of-the-woods, stinkhorn, and reishi are members of different orders, and the silver ear is in a separate taxonomic class called the

Tremellomycetes. Put simply, the cultivated species come from groups of fungi that originated over a vast time span. For comparison, farmed land animals come from only two classes (birds and mammals), and most red meat in grocery stores comes from a single order, the even-toed ungulates, or Artiodactyla (pigs, cattle, sheep, goats). This isn't a watertight thought-experiment, because it is difficult to equate the total genetic diversity among cultivated mushrooms to the cultivated ungulates. Nevertheless, mushrooms have been selected for cultivation from more widely spaced branches on the tree of life.

When we consider what this potpourri of species does, or used to do, in nature, the assortment is less impressive. With few exceptions, all of the cultivated species are wood-decay fungi whose preferred conditions can be reproduced quite easily by feeding their colonies with wood (logs, wood chips, sawdust, or partially digested as manure). Moisture, temperature, and the nitrogen content of the feedstuff are important, but they can be regulated quite easily once the optimal parameters are identified. The button mushroom may be the exception in the list, with wild relatives that may be mycorrhizal, but it does fine on a diet of straw and manure. The picture is very different for the most sought-after wild mushrooms. Again, the species are all over the evolutionary tree, but they live finicky lives involving relationships with living plants and animals: chanterelles and matsutake are mycorrhizal, so they are boletes, and the morels hook up with the roots of trees and shrubs in forest habitats.[19] Chanterelles have been cultivated with pine seedlings in pots. The first report of this method in the 1990s showed a photograph of a solitary fruit body that had poked itself through a drain hole in the base of the pot.[20] Admitting that they had raised only five fruit bodies in their pots, the authors speculated that their method might be perfected and, eventually, applied to matsutake and other valuable species. Fruit bodies of porcini, *Boletus edulis*, can be grown on agar medium but never get big enough to cause excitement in the kitchen. The mycorrhizal relationship may present one of those problems in domestication that can be surmounted only by re-creating most of the original environmental conditions.[21] At some point, even the most ambitious mushroom grower must concede that conservation of mushroom habitats is the only way to grow mushrooms—nature does it better.

Enhancing mushroom fruiting in nature is a different approach to countering the declining harvest of mycorrhizal species. Ascomycete truffles have been cultivated in *truffières* (truffle plantations) since the eighteenth century, and yet the French harvest of black truffles has fallen by more than 95% in the last century.[22] The reasons for the decline are unknown, but climate change is considered a major culprit. Today's truffle growers rely on oak saplings inoculated with specific strains of fungi before planting. Any attempt to cultivate truffles without their natural ecological partners is recognized as a hopeless proposition. Mushroom enthusiasts have not used the same approach to boost the crop of their favorite mycorrhizal basidiomycetes, but there may be some value in promoting wild mushroom growth on deforested land where the original relationships between fungi and trees have been destroyed. This process of trees and fungi participating in the slow redevelopment of productive habitat is an example of bioremediation. The way in which mycorrhizal mushrooms assist the survival of tree seedlings on deforested land and areas damaged by mining, chemical manufacture, exploding nuclear reactors, and other environmental mishaps has been studied from many angles. Mining for coal and nonfuel materials has been a major resource for companies in Ohio, my adopted state, turning forests drained by pristine fishing creeks into highly toxic deserts. Farther east, mountaintop mining is a particularly effective way of ruining the environment that continues to intoxicate the shareholders of coal-mining enterprises in Appalachia. Once the mineral resources have been hauled away, nature is tasked with re-creating the lost Eden, sans mountain, creeks, and so on, but tree seedlings have a difficult time becoming established on ground that is only slightly more hospitable than the surface of the moon. Seedlings inoculated with mycorrhizal fungi seem to do marginally better under these circumstances, presumably because fungal colonies can tap a much larger area of toxic soil for traces of the nutrients that help the trees survive. My cynicism runneth over, but, thankfully, the methodology has a marvelous champion in the form of Paul Stamets, president of the company Fungi Perfecti, in Washington State. He coined the term *mycoremediation* to describe the use of fungi in landscape restoration, and *mycofiltration* for the effectiveness of fungal colonies in cleansing groundwater before it filters into lakes, rivers, and the sea.[23] In addition to partnering with trees, mushroom colonies have proven abilities to detoxify soils. In one experiment, oyster mushroom mycelium was grown on soil that had been blackened by heavy oil. Within one month, the oyster colony had decomposed most of the hydrocarbons and had fruited all over the heap of soil.

Paul Stamets is a well-known evangelist for the potential of growing mushrooms on garbage and believes, in a wider sense, that mushrooms have the potential to save the planet from the ecological catastrophe resulting from the activities of billions of avaricious apes. I am continually amazed by his success in growing mushrooms on unconventional food sources, including coffee grounds and copies of his own books.[24] There is a lot of interest today in growing mushrooms on waste materials from other agricultural processes. Fungi evolved as great recyclers, and one or more species can live on just about every natural product and on plenty of synthetic materials, too. The paddy-straw mushroom, a big white thing whose Latin name is *Volvariella volvacea*, is a particularly adaptable species that can be grown on cotton waste, oil palm, pineapple waste, banana leaves, and, as its common name suggests, rice straw. *Volvariella* is grown in many East Asian and Southeast Asian countries, and much of the harvest is canned for the export market. (As I'll discuss in the next chapter, the fresh fruit bodies resemble the lethal death caps, *Amanita phalloides*, and their relatives, resulting in the poisoning of Asian immigrants in the United States who misidentify one of their native delicacies.)

The edibility of mushrooms grown on such varied materials is an important consideration. Eating fruit bodies that have sprouted from steaming piles of malodorous horse droppings might spoil your appetite (if you were to look at photographs of defecating animals while nibbling on mushroom *vol-au-vents*, for example) but there are no health concerns. Collecting and eating mushrooms from the woods around Chernobyl is another matter. The wide catchment area of soil explored by a mushroom's mycelium means that the fungus can absorb radioactive metals that are widely dispersed in the forest and package them in a concentrated form. Researchers have studied the levels of radioactive cesium-137 (half-life of thirty years) in European mushrooms, and they found significantly higher concentrations in regions affected by the fallout from the reactor disaster. There is a great deal of variability in the radioactivity between mushroom species, and contamination patterns are exceedingly complex. Some commentators are concerned about the export of radioactive mushrooms from Belarus; others suggest that the health risk is insignificant.[25] One study showed that the highest levels of radionuclides were found in mushroom gills, which makes me wonder whether mushrooms release undetermined numbers of radioactive spores.[26] The transfer of isotopes into spores would serve as an effective delivery system for moving radioactive elements into easily respirable microscopic particles.

The fact that people in the most heavily contaminated districts of Ukraine and Belarus continue to collect and consume wild mushrooms testifies to the cultural importance of these fungi. But mushrooms offer surprisingly little nutritional value for the effort expended in picking them. (This augurs well for the sales of my next book, *The 30-Day Mushroom Diet*, which offers a money-back guarantee for rapid skeletification.) A cup of mushrooms contains 15 calories, which isn't much more than those in a serving of lettuce. Like lettuce and other green vegetables, more than 90% of a mushroom is water, with the remaining 10% split between protein and carbohydrate in the form of insoluble fiber. The fat content is negligible. The mixture of vitamins and minerals is unremarkable, with cabbage and brussels sprouts offering more of everything. Little is known about the digestibility of mushrooms, and it is thought that a high proportion of the protein, and of the nonfibrous carbohydrate, may be unavailable for absorption.[27] For this reason, the trifling calorie count may *overestimate* the nutritional value of mushrooms. Of course, calories are not the point. Mushroom enthusiasts—Ukrainian, Belarusian, and otherwise—are enchanted by the flavor and fragrance of wild species, and the less adventuresome enjoy the texture of the toneless button, happily pardoning its failings as a remedy for hunger.

Chapter 6

Death Caps and Muscle Wasters

POISONOUS MUSHROOMS AND
MUSHROOM POISONINGS

Mushrooms are like men—the bad most closely counterfeit the good.

—Paul Gavarni (1804–1866)

I read *Moby Dick* last summer, swiftly, enthralled throughout, following earlier abandoned attempts as a younger and less patient man. The mycological reason for mentioning the greatest novel ever written is that it describes man as a self-imposed victim of nature, which is one way of looking at the phenomenon of mushroom poisoning. But back to Melville for a moment: at the end of the novel, Ahab, driven insane by his hatred for God—who, Ahab has figured out, does not exist—is ensnared by his own harpoon rope and yanked into the sea by poor Moby. Most readers experience relief at this finale. In a similar vein, I often find myself thinking, "Yeah, well done," when I read about a shark tearing a surfer in half, or a mountain lion eviscerating a hiker. Fleetingly, pathetically, the news story assuages my guilt for full personal participation in the destruction of the natural world (as long as, I'm sure, I don't have any personal connection to the victim). In defense of my more charitable nature, I am never thrilled by viral pandemics, waterborne illnesses, or mushroom poisonings. This difference in emotional response may be a reflection of human familiarity with visible, charismatic predators;

we did not evolve with any comprehension of invisible killers. It is difficult, under such historical circumstances, to empathize with a germ or a toxin, whereas a shark that has escaped an Asian cooking pot deserves our universal reverence. (It is a pity, of course, that sharks butcher surfers rather than the people who eat their fins in soup, but that is a peripheral issue.) So, while my scientific training identifies the efficacy of fungal toxins as an indisputable example of the power of natural selection, I do not feel the least celebratory about this aspect of mushroom biology (Fig. 6.1).

Figure 6.1. Detail from frontispiece of G. A. Battarra, *Fungorum Agri Ariminensis Historia* (Faventiae: Typis Ballantiantis, 1755). The translated banner reads, "We look at mushrooms but we don't eat them." Together, the owl and the lynx symbolize thoughtfulness and sharp perception. One of the oldest scientific societies, the Accademia dei Lincei, is named for the lynx. It was founded in 1603 (fifty-nine years before the Royal Society of London) by Federico Cesi, Prince of Acquasparta, who believed that the study of fungal growth and reproduction held the promise of elucidating some of the fundamental mysteries of life. (He was a very insightful man.) Galileo became a member of the Lincei and aided its studies on fungi with the gift of a new instrument for which the academy's secretary, Giovanni Faber, invented the name "microscope."

I'll begin this inquiry with a pair of mushroom species whose ingestion results in speech impairment and a severe backache, followed by the destruction of muscle tissue (causing the victim's urine to turn reddish brown), induction of coma, and eventual heart failure. This abbreviated list of symptoms doesn't recommend the source of the toxins for the dinner table, yet both mushrooms have historically been considered choice edibles: man-on-horseback, or yellow knight—*Tricholoma equestre*—grows in Europe and North America, and *Russula subnigricans* resides in Asia.[1]

Man-on-horseback, known as *Grünling* in Germany and *chevalier* and (more aptly) *canari* in France, is a robust-looking mushroom with a thick yellow stalk, yellow gills, and yellow cap (Plate 12). McIlvaine didn't care for the ones he found in New York State, but authors of more recent guidebooks in North America and in Europe recommend its consumption: "A popular edible," the *Peterson Field Guide* calls it; "excellent," "a good edible," and "a noted delicacy," say a trio of coffee table books on mushrooms; and it is "Edible ++" according to the *Collins Field Guide*.[2] We can't be certain about the etymological link between the mushroom and horsemen, but this seems to have something to do with the impression that the fungus was too good for peasants and should have been reserved for the nobility.[3] In light of this decree, and the assumption that authors of guidebooks are not invested in poisoning their readers, it seems likely that people have enjoyed eating this mushroom for a long time. This *Tricholoma* species is particularly plentiful in France, where it grows in mycorrhizal harmony with pine trees. Despite its supposed safety, a dozen people were hospitalized in Bordeaux and in other parts of the country after eating it in the 1990s. The case histories of the victims were strikingly similar.[4] All of the patients had eaten the same mushrooms in at least three consecutive meals before they developed muscle weakness and myalgia (muscle pain), especially in their legs. Over the next few days, they developed nausea, their muscles weakened, their urine darkened, and their faces reddened. Their blood work showed elevated levels of the activity of an enzyme called serum creatine kinase, which indicates muscle breakdown. Biopsy samples from the patients' leg muscles showed that the myofibrils (the muscle fibers) had a "nibbled" appearance and had become separated from one another with intervening pockets of fluid. Nine of the patients recovered; three died following breathing difficulties, hyperthermia, kidney problems, and cardiovascular collapse. Autopsy revealed damage to muscles in the back, arms, diaphragm, and heart. How could a French gourmet mushroom have done this?

Physicians and scientists studying the cases fed extracts from the *Tricholoma* to mice and watched the same elevation in creatine kinase activity. The treated mice also showed rapid breathing, sluggish activity, and diarrhea, and histological analysis revealed the characteristic disorganization of muscle tissue. The diagnosis for mice and man was rhabdomyolysis: breakdown of muscle fibers. The mice had been fed the human equivalent of 3 kilograms of fresh mushrooms over the course of three days, a significant amount, suggesting that humans were more sensitive to the *Tricholoma* toxins than rodents were. The link between mushroom consumption and muscle damage in both mammals seems irrefutable. A decade later, nobody is sure what toxin caused this, but a potent molecule with the same effects has now been isolated from the myotoxic Asian mushroom, *Russula subnigricans*.

Russula subnigricans has never been showcased as an edible mushroom, but mushroom enthusiasts have eaten it by mistake, and poisonings have been described since the 1950s. Seven known fatalities have occurred in Japan.[5] The symptoms of intoxication are similar to those associated with *Tricholoma equestre* but can begin much sooner, with victims suffering speech impairment and convulsions just a few minutes after ingestion. Japanese chemists have identified the *Russula* toxin as a highly reactive four-carbon compound named *cycloprop-2-ene carboxylic acid.*[6] This has a lethal dose (LD_{100}) of 2.5 milligrams per kilogram body weight, at least for mice. Nature abounds with more powerful toxins, but 1 gram of the *Russula* molecule would suffice to dispatch a dumpster load of mice or a portly string quartet.

The rarity of these muscle poisonings is difficult to understand. If the mushrooms were species that few people encountered, recent cases might be explained by the adventurous nature of modern mushroom pickers. But Europeans have been eating the *Tricholoma* for centuries. By eating the mushrooms over several days, the French victims probably increased the toxin levels in their muscles with each meal. Again, people must have done the same thing in the past, and yet there is no history of poisonings associated with this species. One possibility is that a peculiarly toxic variety of the fungus has been spreading in recent decades. The toxicity of the Asian *Russula* has been known for much longer, but while the fungus is widespread in Japan, all of the poisonings seem to have occurred in the Kyoto area—fruit bodies collected from other regions appear to be safe. Genetic differences between colonies might be a factor, and soil and climatic factors could influence toxicity, too. Regional differences in toxicity may apply to other mushrooms, but does anyone wish to test this by personal experimentation? Even McIlvaine would have declined this challenge.

Adding to the uncertainty about mushroom toxicity, researchers in Finland have reported that all kinds of putatively edible wild mushrooms contain muscle poisons.[7] The investigators came to this conclusion by feeding mushrooms mixed with regular food to female lab mice. Different groups of mice were fed powdered chanterelles, species of *Russula*, boletes, and a polypore called *Albatrellus ovinus*. Irrespective of the mushroom species added to their diets, the mice drank a lot more water and lowered their cholesterol, which seems like a good thing for human mushroom lovers. More disturbingly, they also showed elevated levels of that enzyme, creatine kinase. Although the creatine kinase spike was the signature of rhabdomyolysis, the muscle tissue in the mice looked normal under the microscope. In a follow-up study, the same group reported similar findings in mice fed cultivated button mushrooms, shiitake, and oyster mushrooms.[8] Indeed, they concluded that shiitake was "the most toxic of the studied species," finding liver damage in addition to the biochemical signs of muscle poisoning.

Taken at face value, these findings are alarming. I bet that mushroom growers were not pleased when they read about this research! An important criticism of the Finnish work is that the dosages given to the mice were high—ridiculously high, ranging from the human equivalent of 100 grams of mushrooms to an utterly vomitous 4.5 kilograms per day for five days.[9] This means that all of the readers of this book (yes, both of you) who consume mushrooms regularly are exceedingly unlikely to suffer any harm. The results are still troubling, for a different reason. A variety of mushroom species are consumed in concentrated form as unregulated drugs (softened by the use of the term "medicinals"), marketed to treat everything from loss of libido to terminal cancer. The possibility of widespread myotoxicity of high dosages of mushrooms should be a concern for the producers, marketers, and consumers of these products. (I'll return to medicinal mushrooms in Chapter 8.) Reflecting this anxiety, the researchers noted that the mice that ate the most mushrooms in their study showed the healthiest cholesterol levels: the mushroom dosage with the greatest potential medicinal benefit overlapped with greatest potential toxicity.

Another interesting feature of this study was that a minority of the mushroom-gobbling mice showed no increase in serum creatinase activity at all. Differences in individual physiological responses to chemical compounds produced by mushrooms aren't surprising. The mice in the study varied genetically, though not very much, but also in age and, presumably, in overall health before the study began. Human mushroomers exhibit the same kinds of differences, and these surely affect the outcome of our encounters with poisonous mushrooms, along with other variables, including the amount eaten, the types of food and drink consumed with the mushrooms, and the quality of medical care once symptoms develop. The most compelling feature of the Finnish research is that it encourages a wider inquiry into the distribution of mushroom toxins among the basidiomycetes. The results suggest that toxins may be a lot more common than mushroom guidebooks would lead you to believe. The thing that distinguishes a poisonous listing from "a noted delicacy" may depend upon whether a fungus manufactures its toxins in quantities that are likely to harm us, rather than whether it produces them at all. In addition, the research on *Russula* and *Tricholoma* suggests that the risk of eating a particular species can vary by region. What does all of this say about the value of experts in mushroom identification? This is an important question, because the horrific outcome of a recent poisoning case in Scotland has been blamed, in part, on the paucity of experts in mushroom taxonomy. The victims of this misadventure were a bestselling author and his wife and friends, who found what they thought was a patch of chanterelles.

The webcaps, species of *Cortinarius*, are the most numerous of any genus of mushrooms. The number is debatable, and the current count is certainly on the low side, but experts agree that there are more than 2,000 different species. In Chapter 3, I mentioned that the number of described mushrooms is 16,000, which means that one in every eight mushrooms is a webcap; if that isn't impressive enough, consider that for every species of primate, including lemurs, lorises, galagos, tarsiers, monkeys, and apes, there are five or more different kinds of webcap. The common name for these fungi, and their Latin epithet, refers to the veil of tissue that forms a gauzy sheet beneath the expanding cap, covering the young gills. This is teased apart as the cap gets wider, persisting as a stringy remnant at the top of the stem in some webcaps, leaving no trace in others. The entire genus is mycorrhizal, partnering with conifers and broad-leaved trees. Appearing in all colors, some are edible, including the gypsy mushroom (*Cortinarius caperatus*) and a monster called the goliath webcap (*Cortinarius praestans*), while others are lethal. The toxins produced by the dangerous webcaps are different from the *Russula* muscle poison. They damage kidney tubules, attack the liver, and can wreak havoc in the intestine. Unless you are a webcap, there is nothing to recommend these molecules.

Back to the bestselling author, whose name is Nicholas Evans. If you don't recognize the name, you may remember the movie, *The Horse Whisperer*, based on his book about someone who whispered to horses. I'm not familiar with Mr. Evans' other work, but since the movie grossed $187 million, I am confident he is a lot wealthier than a professor who writes about mushrooms. Now imagine Mr. Evans and his wife picking mushrooms with his brother-in-law, Sir Alastair Gordon-Cumming, and his wife, on the Gordon-Cummings' Scottish estate in 2008. Thinking that they had found some chanterelles, they picked *Cortinarius speciosissimus*, the deadliest webcap, and cooked and ate their harvest (Plate 13). The next day, both couples began feeling ill and were admitted to a local hospital, then transferred to a renal unit in Aberdeen. They received dialysis to try to remove the mushroom toxins from the bloodstream, and while Sir Alastair's wife recovered: the others suffered kidney failure. Two years later, Mr. Evans, his wife, and Sir Alastair are receiving weekly dialysis and the men are waiting for kidney transplants.[10]

Sir Alastair and his wife enjoyed eating wild mushrooms and had often used books to identify fruit bodies they picked on their property. The difference between chanterelles and webcaps is evident to mycologists who know to look at the underside of the cap (chanterelles have ridges rather than the thin straight gills of webcaps), but for someone who has picked edible mushrooms of similar size and color from exactly the same patch of ground on previous occasions, it's easy to mistake one for the other. Contemplating their personal disaster for *The Scotsman*, Sir Alastair said, "…on this occasion we thought it looked like something else. The price of that mistake for my brother-in-law and myself has been pretty catastrophic. However, at least we are still here. People do die."[11]

This was the first documented case of poisoning by *Cortinarius speciosissimus* in Scotland in thirty years,[12] and the involvement of a celebrity author attracted lots of media interest. The timing of the story was interesting in light of the alarm expressed by British mycologists around the same time about the shortage of national expertise in mushroom identification.[13] In the United Kingdom, and elsewhere, there are very few jobs for mycologists who know how to identify different species of mushrooms and other fungi. Mushroom identification can be a lifelong pursuit, and developing skills in this avocation is something that universities and funding agencies are unwilling to support. Various government departments around the world employ small numbers of specialists in fungal taxonomy, but most of these scientists work on agricultural pests. I lead fungal forays in Ohio, Kentucky, and Pennsylvania from time to time but can only discriminate with confidence between the common species. My limitations in this arena are shared by the majority of my professional colleagues. Despite the lack of funding, the skills haven't disappeared entirely and are being cultivated by amateur mycologists who draw upon a wealth of experience to recognize the often subtle characteristics of fruit bodies that distinguish species. My friend Michael Kuo, who teaches English at Eastern Illinois University, is a passionate amateur mycologist. Here's what Michael says about confronting a *Russula*:

> When I try to identify russulas, I don't even bother if I don't have at least three specimens to work with (unless there is something *very* distinctive about the mushroom), representing the various stages of maturity. I carefully record all of the ridiculous features—like how far the cap cuticle peels, or whether the spores are "partially" or "completely" reticulate—to the best of my ability, trying to be objective. I have found that it helps to curse loudly while doing this, but this may or may not help you with the process. Then I get out the keys and descriptions, and have at it. I keep my expectations low, because I know that I am likely to end up with three or four possibilities, each of which varies fairly substantially on one or another feature.[14]

There is nothing boastful about the title of Michael's website, MushroomExpert.com: few rival his skills in mushroom identification. The scarcity of his kind of knowledge is troubling for a number of reasons, but I'm not convinced that the paucity of Scottish mushroom experts translates into problems in treating poisonings. A mycologist who consulted on the Scottish cases said, "If somebody had been able to identify [the mushroom] within a few hours of eating it, or getting to hospital, maybe we would have been able to save their kidneys."[15] If Nicholas Evans and Sir Alastair had been bitten by a venomous snake or a spider, the identity of the animal might have been critical, because physicians have a choice between different antivenoms. But there are no proven antidotes for mushroom poisoning, and the treatment of patients depends upon the severity of the poisoning symptoms, not upon the fungal species. There is certainly an advantage to knowing what mushroom a patient has eaten—if, for example, someone suffering from intestinal distress is known to have eaten inkcaps rather than webcaps, they can be told that their illness will wane without treatment—but by the time symptoms of life-threatening mushroom poisoning develop, usually not long before the patient shows up at the hospital, the treatment is the same regardless of the species. Mushroom poisoning is, unfortunately, akin to a stab wound: the treatment isn't predicated on the type of knife. The practical value in knowing how to tell mushrooms apart lies in preventing people from eating toxic species in the first place. Whether mushroom pickers are taught what to look for by an amateur or a professional mycologist doesn't matter to me, as long as the information is accurate.

In addition to people who pick in search of ever more flavorful recipes, magic mushroomers are a second group of potential poisoning victims who would benefit from a weekend course on mushroom identification. Echoing the Scottish cases, four young men in Germany suffered kidney failure after eating webcaps that they had hoped were hallucinogenic liberty caps, *Psilocybe semilanceata*.[16] Magic mushroomers are particularly vulnerable because they tend to eat so many fresh mushrooms in recreational pursuit of altered perceptions. The dose of three to six liberty caps recommended by devotees amounts to a squishy handful of mushroom tissue; the same number of misidentified toxic webcaps weighs a lot more and would ruin the career of my aforementioned and luckless string quartet.

The treatment of all forms of mushroom poisoning has improved through attention to patient hydration and maintenance of the electrolyte balance in the bloodstream. In rare instances, when patients are admitted to the hospital within a few hours of eating mush-rooms, they can benefit from induced vomiting or stomach pump-ing, aspiration of the small intestine (using a tube slid through the nose), and charcoal ingestion (to reduce toxin absorption from the intestine). When someone has eaten the most damaging kinds of mushrooms, including webcaps and death caps, symptoms can be delayed for days after the meal—by the time the victim arrives at the hospital, the toxins have already been absorbed. Dialysis has become a more common therapy in recent years, particularly in the United States, and it can remove toxins from the bloodstream before they destroy the kidneys and liver. Early dialysis is the key to the treat-ment's success. Some experts also recommend administering a drug called N-acetylcysteine along with high doses of penicillin to protect against kidney failure, but the efficacy of these drugs is unproven.[17]

The ferocity of *Cortinarius* against the kidneys and liver is prob-ably due to the blood-purifying functions of these organs. The toxins are probably capable of damaging tissues in other parts of the body, but these effects are obscured by their rapid concentra-tion in the kidney tubules and the liver. The delay between eating the mushrooms and the onset of symptoms is one of the distinc-tive features of webcap poisoning. The largest doses of the toxins are manifested by severe kidney damage within two days, whereas less serious cases can remain "silent" for an astonishing three weeks after the mushroom meal. The poisonous nature of webcaps wasn't recognized until the 1950s, when a Polish epidemiologist discov-ered that *Cortinarius orellanus* (a relative of the species implicated in the Scottish cases) was responsible for a poisoning epidemic that affected more than 100 people and resulted in 11 deaths.[18] The webcaps contain many compounds that are thought to be toxic, but there is some disagreement about which one, or which ones, cause kidney failure. We know the most about *orellanine*, named by the

Polish investigator after the mushroom he indicted. Its chemical structure resembles paraquat and other herbicides whose inadvisable ingestion also cause kidney damage. Other toxicologists argue that molecules called *cortinarins* are more dangerous. Cortinarins are examples of cyclopeptides (rings of amino acids) and resemble the structure of the lethal amatoxins produced by death caps, destroying angels, and related species of *Amanita*.

The toxicity of death caps and their kin has been recognized for millennia, for as long, no doubt, as humans, or earlier social hominids with enough smarts to point and frown (or burst into tears), have eaten mushrooms. According to Pliny and other classical writers, Emperor Claudius I was murdered by his fourth wife, who added poisonous mushrooms to his favorite meal: the beautiful orange-capped species we call Caesar's mushroom, *Amanita caesarea*. Most scholars have assumed that the weapon was the death cap, *Amanita phalloides* (Plate 14). Others have suggested that the death caps might have been collected by mistake and served to the emperor without malice, or that Claudius was served a dish of porcini or ceps, *Boletus edulis*, laced with poison.[19] One aspect of the story is undeniable: death caps are very, very, very poisonous.

The lethal toxins in death caps are called amatoxins.[20] They are synthesized by other kinds of mushrooms, including a little brown species called the deadly galerina, *Galerina marginata* (identified as *Galerina autumnalis* in many guidebooks), which has caused poisonings among mushroomers searching for hallucinogenic *Psilocybe* mushrooms. The fruit bodies are small, with caps no larger than bottle caps, but determined pickers may find and eat enough of them to suffer long-term damage. The death cap, *Amanita phalloides*, and its poisonous relatives are much larger, beautiful firm-fleshed fruit bodies with clean surfaces that almost demand to be eaten, particularly if the picker has been used to eating mushrooms with a similar appearance. The death cap often has a greenish hue, but the destroying angel, *Amanita bisporigera*, is pure white and looks quite similar to the cultivated paddy-straw mushroom, *Volvariella volvacea*, described in the previous chapter. The paddy-straw mushroom is a popular species in Asia, and many of the victims of amanitin poisoning in North America come from immigrant families that take an *Amanita* home for dinner. The situation may be aggravated by the fact that the death cap is an invasive species that appears to have been spreading in California in recent decades.[21]

Amatoxins are cyclopeptide molecules, like cortinarins produced by webcaps, that inhibit the activity of an enzyme called RNA polymerase II that is crucial for protein synthesis. Robbed of this catalyst, the liver stops working, and livers are not as easily transplanted as the kidneys of webcap-poisoned mushroomers. The toxicity of one of the amatoxins called alpha-amanitin is extraordinary. A single cap contains a few thousandths of a gram, enough to kill the fittest of my musicians; 1 gram, the weight of a sweetener packet, would silence an entire symphony orchestra. Like webcaps, a hefty meal of *Amanita* provokes vomiting within a few hours. If people seek medical care immediately, and physicians are able to determine that death caps or their relatives have been eaten, aggressive treatment may be successful. This opportunity is often missed because the early gastrointestinal phase is followed by a two- or three-day "honeymoon" in which the patient feels better. During this time, the amatoxins circulate in the bloodstream and cause damage to the liver and other organs. Three days after the meal, symptoms of liver failure are obvious in severe poisonings.

No one would eat death caps knowingly, right? Wrong! Allow me to introduce Dr. Pierre Bastien, a French physician who ate a whole fruit body in 1974. Having survived, he ate another six years later.[22]

In the 1950s and 60's, Bastien had treated fifteen victims of death-cap poisoning with intravenous injections of vitamin C (morning and evening) and oral doses of two kinds of antibiotic (three times a day). With greater attention to gastronomy than toxicology, I suspect, Pierre specified that the only food allowed during the treatment was carrot soup. All of his patients recovered. Bastien attracted considerable publicity by demonstrating the effectiveness of his therapy on himself, but the technique was never embraced by the medical community. The infrequency of cases and ethical difficulties in deciding who would receive vitamins and antibiotics versus placebos have precluded the randomized trials needed to properly test his method. In the meantime, mushroomers are injured by amatoxins every year. The blessed milk thistle, *Silybum marianum*, is the source of a drug called *silibinin* that was approved for use in Germany in 1984 for treating amatoxin poisoning. There is a body of anecdotal evidence that injections of silibinin can protect liver cells against damage by amatoxins, and approval for use in the United States is pending the results of a clinical trial in California.[23]

Compared to ravages caused by the muscle-wasting, kidney-destroying, and liver-ravaging toxins synthesized by basidiomycetes, other illnesses that have been tied to particular mushrooms are a proverbial walk in the park. The common inkcap, *Coprinopsis atramentaria*, produces an inhibitor of ethanol metabolism, treating unwary human predators to symptoms of alcohol poisoning. The deliberate consumption of the fly agaric, *Amanita muscaria*, for its inebriating qualities causes unwelcome confusion, dizziness, and hallucinations in some party animals, resulting in hospital admission.[24] (The chemistry of the fly agaric will be featured in the next chapter.) The false morel, *Gyromitra esculenta*, is an ascomycete, but it qualifies as a "mushroom" based on its elaboration of fat stalk bearing a convoluted brainoid head. It produces a compound called gyromitrin that is metabolized to form monomethylhydrazine, also known as rocket fuel. Gastrointestinal symptoms occur within hours of the meal, but most people recover within a few days. False morels can be eaten if they are boiled two or more times, discarding the water each time, while making sure that the kitchen is well ventilated to allow the volatile toxin to evaporate. Captain McIlvaine advised his readers to avoid these fungi, but they have attracted modern fanatics who rate them as some of the best edible mushrooms on earth. Enthusiasts call them "beefsteaks" in the Midwest and eat them without any concern about their potential toxicity. Other mushrooms may sicken people, but these species are eaten so rarely, or cause problems for such a small proportion of consumers, that we remain uncertain about their safety.

Stories about lethal mushrooms grab our attention every year and may give the impression that mushroom poisoning is a widespread problem. It isn't—the vast majority of mushroomers don't put anything in their mouths they aren't sure about. The annual tally of reported mushroom poisonings in the United States in the last five years ranges from 5,644 to 8,821.[25] The statistics for 2008 show that the mushrooms were not identified in 79% of the cases and that the vast majority of patients suffered nothing more than mild symptoms. Among the 1,171 cases in which the type of mushroom was identified, hallucinogenic fungi accounted for half of all hospital visits. Some individuals had become disturbed by their hallucinations, others by gastrointestinal distress that may have been caused by bacteria that thrive on the surface of the fruit bodies. That leaves 600 instances of bona fide mushroom poisoning out of a population of more than 300 million people. There were a total of four deaths from eating mushrooms in 2008: three due to *Amanita* and one caused by an unidentified species. Considering that more than 9,000 Americans were poisoned by toilet bowl cleaning agents,

70,000 by stings and bites from jellyfish, insects, spiders, snakes, and other animals, and another 200,000 by swallowing cosmetics and personal care products (including toothpaste), it is difficult to become outraged by the lack of public- or private-sector investment in the profession of mushroom identification.

Mycologists lack a satisfactory theory for the meaning of mushroom toxins—we don't have a clear explanation for the reason that mushrooms produce such poisonous chemicals. It is possible that they are byproducts of the frenetic metabolism of the colony and fruit body and that their toxicity confers no selective advantage to the fungus. A sensible alternative is that the toxins protect mushrooms by working as chemical antipredators or antifeedants (which amount to the same thing). Following this line of inquiry, the stimulus for mushroom toxicity surely lies with the invertebrates—the hordes of insects, nematodes, and other critters most likely to devour the flesh of the fungus. A handful of experiments support this model, with studies on *Drosophila*, or fruit flies, indicating sensitivity to mushroom toxins among flies that breed in fleshy fruits and tolerance among species that feed and lay eggs in mushrooms.[26] This antifeedant explanation of mushroom toxicity is confused by the observation that most species aren't poisonous—how do edible mushrooms survive the rapacious beasties in the woods? The caps of many of the boletes teem with the larvae of flies and other insects, but there are no obvious differences in the level of infestation between edible species and the handful of poisonous boletes. *Russula* species, edible or otherwise, are often insect-free, but their bright caps are scalloped by the radulas of browsing slugs and snails. The important point here is that skull-and-crossbones symbols in guidebooks do not translate into any obvious patterns of toxicity toward other animals. Chemists have identified the toxins that cause the greatest number of human poisonings, but they haven't begun to catalog the galaxy of compounds that kill embryonic insects and dissuade their mothers from laying eggs in caps in the first place.

Irrespective of the details of the interactions between mushrooms and animals, none of today's mushroom species would be here unless their ancestors had been successful at making fruit bodies and releasing spores throughout their evolutionary history. If the pests had triumphed, the mushroom's genes would have been pruned from the biosphere forever. Relationships between mushrooms and insect larvae probably involve the kind of continuous push-and-shove that is characteristic of predators and their prey. An insect that causes too much damage to mushroom caps might lose its nesting place by preventing reproduction of the fungus. And a mushroom might be better served by "allowing" a modest level of infestation rather than making an energy-sapping metabolic investment in making a fruit body that is so toxic that nothing would ever touch it. Mushrooms could not have survived and diversified over tens of millions of years without careful management of their enemies. But it is unlikely that any mushroom toxins are directed against us. Humans are such a recent invention that little of nature has been sculpted with us in mind. For most of our history we have posed no specific threat to mushrooms; we have been effective at destroying natural habitats and causing desertification for thousands of years, but until the advent of commercial mushroom hunting we haven't endangered mushrooms by eating them. The longer tenure of other mammals has provided more opportunity for mushrooms to elaborate antifeedants against our hairy and nippled relatives and it has been suggested that the hallucinogenic "toxins" in the fly agaric are synthesized for this purpose.[27] I suppose these chemicals might work as a deterrent for non-human fungivores, but evolution hasn't had long enough to try a different tack in light of our species' desire for mind-altering experiences (see Chapter 7). Far from working as an antifeedant, the presence of these alkaloids is the only reason that anyone has ever deliberately eaten a fly agaric! On a wider note, hallucinogens and other delayed-action drugs seem like poor devices for discouraging feeding. Author to mushroom: Make something bitter so they spit you out.

Whether or not we are the intended targets of any mushroom toxins, it is interesting, and of potential practical benefit, to determine if mushrooms possess a suite of recognizable characteristics that separate the noxious from the edible.[28] Rather than analyzing folklore about toadstools that blacken silver spoons, et cetera, researchers have looked carefully at coloration and odor. The reasoning behind this is that a mushroom that signals its nastiness to potential predators would avoid a lot of damage. An obvious model is the warning coloration of butterflies that advertises their unpalatability. In a study of guidebook descriptions of more than 500 species of fungi, investigators found no associations between fruit body toxicity and color. But they did find that poisonous species showed a stronger tendency to produce distinctive odors. The limitations of a study of guidebook descriptions are obvious: they only list colors and odors that *we* find distinctive. I bet that a pregnant insect and a mycologist hold very different opinions about the attractiveness of a mushroom's scent and color.

Throughout the history of mycology, investigators captivated by the beauty and strangeness of fruit bodies have sought to overcome the deep-seated squeamishness that many cultures have developed toward fungi. The Flemish priest van Sterbeeck pioneered the acceptance of mushrooms in his seventeenth-century work, *Theatrum Fungorum* (Chapter 4); unperturbed by poisoning himself and his family with mushrooms (Chapter 1), Worthington Smith published a colorful chart comparing edible and poisonous mushrooms in the nineteenth century (Chapter 1), and Captain McIlvaine risked his life to test the limits of mushroom edibility for his American country-men at the turn of the twentieth century (Chapter 4). These attempts to popularize mushroom consumption were surely more successful in promoting the study of fungi than in changing anyone's diet. Wide variations in the cultural acceptance of mushrooms persist to this day. The stark contrast between the traditional mistrust of mush-rooms by the British and the love of wild mushrooms by Russians and other Eastern Europeans is the classic example. Beyond Europe, there is similar diversity of mushroom appreciation, with many Asian cultures revering edible fungi for thousands of years, while others ignore the fungi in their environment.[29] But even in the most myco-philic countries, people express understandable revulsion toward death caps. This reaction was exploited by an American creationist in the 1920s who opposed the teaching of evolution in a book titled *The Toadstool Among the Tombs* (Fig. 6.2),[30] which depicted biolo-gists as a poisonous influence on society. A Nazi propagandist did the same thing when he equated Jews with poisonous mushrooms in a series of illustrated children's stories.[31] Emily Dickinson likened mushrooms to Judas in her poem "Mushroom," which closes:

> Had nature any outcast face,
> Could she a son contemn,
> Had nature an Iscariot,
> That mushroom,—it is him.

> (Dickinson, "Mushroom," stanza 5)[32]

In an online post, a Christian fundamentalist compared the decep-tive beauty of "a deadly toadstool" with the teachings of other religions, and fungi have also been used as symbols for the multi-tude of crimes against the church for which women are—wholly,

Fig. 6.2 Illustration from cover of B. H. Shadduck, *The Toadstool Among the Tombs* (B. H. Shadduck, 1925) that depicted biologists—particularly evolutionary biologists—as a poisonous influence on society.

unreservedly, and obviously—responsible.[33] Mushrooms are similarly abused in commentaries and cartoons dealing with secular issues whenever, for example, a government is depicted as a parasitic and rapidly expanding entity.

Less frequently, mushrooms are celebrated for their dynamism.[34] In her "Mushrooms," Sylvia Plath described the steady, inconspicuous development of the fungus before its glorious fruiting as a metaphor for patience and self-possession, assertiveness, and activism. The poem ends with these lines:

Nudgers and shovers
In spite of ourselves.
Our kind multiplies:

We shall by morning
Inherit the earth.
Our foot's in the door.

(Plath, "Mushrooms," lines 28–33)[35]

Other writers have reveled in the joy of mushroom hunting—mushrooms play a major role in romantic scenes in *Anna Karenina* and Barbara Kingsolver's *Prodigal Summer*.[36] In the majority of poems and novels, however, authors use fungi metaphorically to indicate danger, death, and decay.[37] Shelley's well-known poem, *The Sensitive Plant*, published in 1820, illustrates this with his portrait of inkcaps, which "Started like mist from the wet ground cold," and whose "moss rotted off them, flake by flake," before "Infecting the winds that wander by." Fungi are nature's morticians, and the phenomenon of terminal mushroom poisoning, however rare, is a reliably unsettling fact of life. This is a big part of the ancient superstitions about mushrooms and their supernatural powers. The peculiar bioluminescence of mushrooms like the jack-o-lanterns, *Omphalotus illudens* and its relatives, is an additional source of wonderment.[38] It is, however, the hallucinatory properties of magic mushrooms that have done more than anything to paint the fungi as the strangest part of nature, transforming the spore-shedding organs of subterranean microbes into the playthings of the modern shroomer and the sorcerer's link to the divine.

Chapter 7

The Victorian Hippie

MORDECAI COOKE AND THE SCIENCE OF MUSHROOM INTOXICATION

A young man came to see me in my university office a few years ago, having heard about my research program from one of my students. Rejecting my offer of an armchair as some kind of unfathomable joke, he insisted upon sitting on the floor. This man who laughed at my furniture didn't strike me as dangerous, but his level of agitation was alarming. Grinning, he unzipped his backpack, revealing a copy of *Mr. Bloomfield's Orchard*, furtively displaying it as though it were a work of rare pornography. His hands were shaking. Rummaging in his backpack again, he withdrew a bottle of vodka, from which he took a slug. I closed my office door, fearing the intrusion of my colleagues more than the future actions of this unusual visitor. He jabbered about mushrooms, proclaiming his passion for all things mycological, with particular emphasis upon the miraculous shrooms that transported him far from his twenty-first-century trials. I asked him how he came by his psilocybes, and this made him laugh more than the armchair had. Pulling a digital camera from his pocket, he showed me photographs of his growing room, a basement filled with lamps on chains suspended over trays that spawned thousands of fruit bodies. He was a local grower, dealer, and ardent user. Mushrooms were his life. He asked me why I was interested in fungi. I told him a little about some experiments on spores, though I'm not confident he heard me over the turmoil in his head. He left in a great hurry, and I never saw him again.

There was a time when I toyed with the idea of eating magic mushrooms, but despite my fascination with fungi, I have never experimented with them in this way. My decision was not one of morals or squeamishness: I smoked plenty of weed in my teens before tiring of its effects. No, the choice was predicated upon great spiritual shallowness. I have never wanted to see things differently—the woods in springtime have always appeared stunning, almost overpowering my senses—and now, in middle age, I tolerate my personal psychiatric prescription of vague contentment, fleeting joy, and incurable thanatophobia. In full comprehension of the eternity of nothingness in my future, I want to avoid feeling at one with my surroundings for as long as possible. I thought it useful to get this out of the way before I begin writing about magic mushrooms, given that some of you are better qualified to describe what it feels like to have a mushroom reprogram your senses. This explains why I will try to stick with the *science* of mushroom intoxication, rather than the *experience*, following the tradition of an unusual mycologist named Mordecai Cooke.

Born to Baptist parents in Norfolk, Mordecai Cubitt Cooke (1825–1914), who preferred to be called "M.C."—or "M.C.C.," sharing initials with England's famous cricket club—was steeped in natural history during childhood rambles with his younger brother, William, and while collecting wildflowers with his mother.[1] My introduction to the natural world wasn't so different, which I know sounds ridiculous to anyone born after 1980. Children in rural areas, the fortunate ones, used to grow up playing outdoors, climbing trees, chasing insects, building dens, and so on. There were no video games; televisions had valves, and, once warmed, broadcast discussions about declining standards with white men in suits who had degrees from Oxford or Cambridge. The outdoors had zero competition. Mordecai's acquaintance with fungi began with puff-balls (children would puff them in one another's faces) and handling pieces of rotting "touchwood" lit by bioluminescent mycelia. After village schooling, Cooke was tutored by an uncle who furthered his botanical education. At fifteen, he began training as a draper's assistant, sang and played the flute for choral societies and bands organized by the Temperance Movement, and shot birds on the Norfolk marshes, which were stuffed and sold as decorations for Victorian drawing rooms. Later, he worked as an apothecary's assistant and then as a copying clerk in London, published pamphlets with romantic titles, lectured on poetry, and married a spinster who had an illegitimate daughter. After losing his clerking job, he moved his family to Birmingham and became a teacher in a boys' school. There is nothing in this early biography to suggest that Cooke would become a countercultural hero, but he published a very peculiar book in 1860, when he resigned, or was fired, from the school.

The Seven Sisters of Sleep: Popular History of the Seven Prevailing Narcotics of the World was a study of tobacco, opium, *Cannabis*, betel leaves and areca nuts, coca leaves, *Datura* and other narcotic relatives of the potato plant, and the fly agaric mushroom.[2] Discourse on this catalog of natural products was underpinned by Cooke's thesis that humans have a universal desire for mood-altering drugs and will always find plants in their environment that get the job done. Tobacco was given the most detailed treatment, reflecting Cooke's passion for smoking. According to Andy Letcher in his splendid book *Shroom*,[3] Cooke took the idea of the origins of native narcotic use from an earlier book by a Scottish agricultural chemist, James Johnston, titled *The Chemistry of Common Life*.[4] Cooke took a good deal more than this from Johnston's book: *The Seven Sisters of Sleep* was little more than an unacknowledged retelling of Johnston's work, and many of its passages are pure plagiarism. There were a few differences between the authors' approaches to the subject. Johnston's prose reflected national perceptions about the elevation of the British above the great unwashed of other nations: "It is from such effects of this substance [*hashish, or resin from Indian hemp*] also that we obtain a solution of the extravagances and barbarous cruelties which we read of as practiced occasionally by Eastern despots." (Written at a time when the British were behaving, of course, with unvarying decency throughout their colonies.) And, "This drug [*hashish again*] seems, in fact, to be to the oriental a source of exquisite and *peculiar* enjoyment, which unfits him for the ordinary affairs of this rough life, and with which happily we are, in this part of the world, still altogether unacquainted." By contrast, Cooke reveled in the pleasures and international diversity of drug use: "In Asia Minor an extract from the Indian hemp has been from time immemorial swallowed with the greatest avidity, as the means of producing the most ecstatic delight, and affording a gratification even of a higher character than that which is known there to follow on the use of opium." Additionally, referring to fly agarics, "this intoxication is affirmed to be, not only cheap, which is a consideration, but also remarkably pleasant." Cooke went further, admonishing his countrymen for their double standards in decrying opium use while enjoying cigars. His was a surprisingly optimistic thesis on mankind, extinguished in our century by the horrors of the global drug trade.

Drawing upon reports from explorers in Siberia, and on the Kamchatka Peninsula in the Russian Far East, Cooke recounted the effects of fly agarics, including the common occurrence of "Erroneous impressions of size and distance." We know now that these illusions are caused by a pair of alkaloids in flesh of the fruit body, ibotenic acid and muscimol, that cross the blood-brain barrier, interfere with the normal transmission of nerve impulses, and elevate levels of serotonin and dopamine (Fig. 7.1).[5] Cooke noted that a love of the fly agaric had developed in Russia, where the climate militated against the natural growth or cultivation of the kinds of narcotic plants described in the rest of his book. Discovering that the active agents in the mushroom retained some of their potency after absorption in the gut and passage through the kidneys, inebriates apparently collected and drank their mushroom-infused urine when fresh fruit bodies were in short supply. Cooke obtained this unsavory information from Johnston, who had drawn upon earlier accounts of mushroom use that came from the pen of a Swedish cartographer, Philip Johan von Strahlenberg, who traveled in Siberia and Kamchatka in the early eighteenth century.[6]

Whether Oxford don Charles Dodgson (aka Lewis Carroll) fantasized about the prepubescent Alice Liddell drinking hallucinogenic urine is a matter for serious scholars. He did have Alice gulp from a bottle labeled "DRINK ME," causing her to shrink, before introducing her to the hookah-smoking caterpillar on his mushroom in *Alice's Adventures in Wonderland*. The alternately irritable

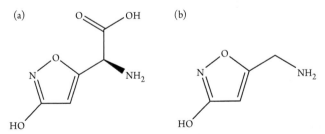

Figure 7.1. Chemical structure of hallucinogenic compounds in *Amanita muscaria*, the fly agaric (a) ibotenic acid, (b) muscimol. Muscimol binds to the $GABA_A$ receptor altering neuronal activity in the cerebral cortex, hippocampus, and cerebellum.

Source: Images courtesy of Diana Davis.

and laid-back larva explains to Alice that different sides of the mushroom cap will make her taller and shorter. After experimenting with morsels from right and left, Alice nibbles from the shrink-me side of the cap, causing her to telescope to 9 inches before meeting the Duchess and the grinning Cheshire Cat. Tim Burton's extravagant use of mushrooms in his movie *Alice*, goes far beyond the single fruit body featured in Carroll's work, with forests of fungi dwarfing the characters in Wonderland. Jules Verne described giant chthonic mushrooms in his 1864 classic, *Journey to the Center of the Earth*, and a similar scene appeared in *Etidorhpa*, an eventual best-seller written by John Uri Lloyd, elder brother of the eccentric Cincinnati mycologist.[7] Lloyd's book, whose title is Aphrodite backwards, describes a journey by a gentleman under the guidance of an eyeless freak of uncertain gender through a subterranean forest of towering mushrooms (Fig. 7.2). Lacking clothes, hair, and visible genitalia, the tour guide resembles a modern luge athlete in the book's illustrations, and the journeyman looks a bit like Charles Darwin. The forest was reached via a cave in Kentucky that opened to a hollow planetary interior.[8]

It isn't clear whether Carroll came up with the idea of changing Alice's size before he had considered introducing a mushroom into his story. Nor has the source of his knowledge about hallucinogenic mushrooms been pinned down. Cooke's description of the fly agaric's mind-bending properties is one possibility: "a straw in the road becomes a formidable object, to overcome which a leap is taken sufficient to clear a barrel of ale." Provocatively, the pages of the fly agaric chapter are the only ones to have been cut open in the copy of *The Seven Sisters* in the Bodlean Library, and we know that this book was there when Carroll made his only recorded visit, in 1862.[9] It is equally likely that he was intrigued by tales of hallucinogenic mushrooms told by other Victorian writers.

Figure 7.2. "Forest of colossal fungi," by John Augustus Knapp published in J. U. Lloyd, *Etidorhpa* (Cincinnati: J. U. Lloyd, 1895).

The subject of *The Seven Sisters* was not at all representative of Mordecai Cooke's later writings. He went on to publish hundreds of books and articles on fungi, was active in numerous scientific societies, worked at Kew Gardens, and was a founding member of the British Mycological Society in 1896. Cooke's domestic arrangements were less conventional: his stepdaughter, Annie, bore his first child at eighteen years old and had seven more before leaving him in her early forties. His wife seems to have supported this *ménage á trois,* playing grandmother to Mordecai's children.[10] Cooke paid Annie an allowance once she left home, but his sadness at her absence and the financial strain of supporting two households made for a troubled retirement.

If we limit Cooke's biography to the drug book and his unconscionable relationship with his stepdaughter, it is possible to view him as a kind of reprehensible Victorian hippie, a heavily bearded deviant who authored *The Celebrated Drug Classic*—the subtitle of a recent edition of *The Seven Sisters*.[11] Yet, there is little in this strange man's obsessive work habits, in most of his vast catalog of writings, and in his reserved nature that recommend him as any kind of counterculture father. In fact, in a later book, *Edible and Poisonous Fungi: What to Eat and What to Avoid*, published by the Society for Promoting Christian Knowledge, Cooke warned "all eaters of toadstools against experiments with the brilliant Fly Mushroom."[12] Half a century after his death, however, there was still plenty of interest in the psychedelic mushrooms whose effects he had been among the first to describe.

There seems little point in spilling much ink on Robert Gordon Wasson (1898–1986) when he spent so much time documenting his own mycological investigations in such painful detail. I'll offer only a couple of paragraphs on this gentleman, for whom mycology was a distraction from his work as vice president of J. P. Morgan, and refer you again to Andy Letcher's masterful *Shroom* for more detailed analysis.

Sixteenth-century conquistadors' accounts of mushroom use in the religious festivals of the Mesoamerican civilizations they annihilated, and mushroom motifs in the ancient stonework and illustrations in Mixtec chronicles, provide glimpses of a lengthy history of hallucinogenic mushroom use in Latin America. In the 1950s, Wasson thought he had discovered remnants of these cultural practices in Mexico, when he recorded the intoxicated ramblings of a woman called María Sabina who may, or may not, have been a shaman. (There is no degree certificate to prove one's credentials as a shaman, of course, but Letcher reveals some troubling inconsistencies in her biography.) If you have many hours to kill, I recommend listening to the interminable chanting of María.[13] You can even sing and groan along with the lady by following the published transcript and musical score.

Based on my training in anthropology (nonexistent), I conclude with a high degree of certainty that she made lots of the stuff up as she rambled along, drawing upon fragments of Catholicism and other meaningless ideas that occurred to her as she became exceedingly high. During the recordings, you can hear some of the celebrants clearing their throats, spitting with vengeance, and, later, vomiting and violent nose blowing. Here's a brief excerpt from the transcript:

> Woman of the whirlpool in the lake am I, woman who waits am I,
> Woman who tries am I, clean woman am I,
> Oh Jesus, my patron Mother, look at this world,
> Look how it is, dangerous world, dark world,
> I'm going to free this, [the mushroom] says, I'm going to dry it
> out in the sunlight, [the mushroom] says,
> Woman of the hunting dog am I.[14]

And on, and on, hour after unbearable hour. Wasson's studies might be understandable if he had been out of his head when he listened to all of this rubbish, but his fascination with María did not dim when he was sober, illustrating, I suppose, the appalling monotony of a career in the financial industries.

The mushrooms consumed by Sabina and her disciples were species of *Psilocybe*, rather than fly agarics (Plate 15). The term "magic mushroom," coined by Wasson, isn't applied to fly agarics but is reserved for the handful of mushroom genera that contain hallucinogenic alkaloids called psilocybin and psilocin. Paul Stamets, president of *Fungi Perfecti*, a company based in Olympia, Washington, is an expert on *Psilocybe* mushrooms and offers the following guide to their identification: "If a gilled mushroom has purplish brown to black spores, *and* the flesh bruises bluish, the mushroom in question is very likely a psilocybin-producing species."[15] The majority of psilocybin-producers are species of *Psilocybe* and *Panaeolus*. There are almost 400 species of *Psilocybe* and one in four contain psilocybin; most of the 100 species of *Panaeolus* fruit on herbivore dung and about one in ten are hallucinogenic. The taxonomy of these mushrooms is in turmoil in light of genetic studies that are carving the bluing *Psilocybe* species away into a separate genus of hallucinogenic fungi. In the future, mycologists may refer to all of the best-known *Psilocybe* species as kinds of *Weraroa*, a nomenclatural necessity that will likely be ignored by shroomers. Incidentally, these magic mushrooms seem to be related to the genus *Galerina*, including the deadly galerina, *Galerina marginata*, which contains amatoxins (Chapter 6).

After ingestion, psilocybin is converted into psilocin, which is thought to be the psychoactive compound. Psilocin is similar in chemical structure to serotonin, and when it reaches the brain it docks with a pair of serotonin receptors and upsets the normal functioning of the neocortex (Fig. 7.3).[16] The neocortex, or cerebral cortex, is the outer layer of the mammalian brain, the evolutionary add-on of 100 billion neurons in humans that persuades billions of us that we are more important than the rest of nature. Higher mental functions, such as reasoning, language, and consciousness, operate in the neocortex; the neocortex is also responsible for sensory perception and is the source of our motor commands. Serotonin receptors control the release of all kinds of neurotransmitters and hormones, which explains the intensity of the experiences of shroomers, or self-proclaimed "psychonauts." Here's a description of the *Psilocybe* trip from Paul Stamets:

> ... under the full force of mushrooms, the heavens open up with
> a full display of beauty hard to describe. Visual acuity is enhanced
> to the point where the sky becomes three dimensional.... The

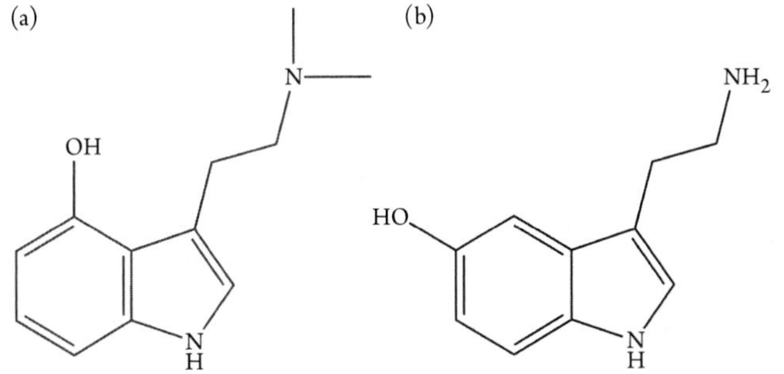

Figure 7.3. Similarity in chemical structure between (a) psilocin and (b) serotonin. Psilocin binds to a pair of serotonin receptors.

Source: Images courtesy of Diana Davis.

universe moves in harmony. My spirit moves with it. I feel as though I have become a thread in the fabric of nature and have returned home.[17]

Stamets reflects emotional responses to *Psilocybe* that are common to many practitioners. A number of websites allow people to post their mushroom experiences, and the following examples from www.magic-mushrooms.net offer a good indication of the overall content:

I started seeing flashing lights that no one else could see and my mate saw a huge ring of light with a black hole inside it. It was Great.

Every one of us had the sensation that things were split into little blocks like mosaics, and these were just buzzing around. Our faces were doing that, the walls were doing that, everything. We all had the sensation of being in the "matrix" surrounded by, what felt like, tangible air. Almost like you could reach out and touch it. At the same time, we lost all sense of self. Didn't know how to interact or do something as simple as make a slice of toast!!!!

The descriptions' sameness suggests a common suite of disturbances to the nervous system. "Didn't know how to...make a slice of toast!!!!" is probably the most original item of self-reflection that I encountered in a half-hour of Googling around the shroom sites. Mushroom trips can obviously have a profound effect upon the perceptions of individuals and may make them considerably happier, but it is important to recognize that each trip is a personal response to the changes in perception caused by psilocybin. Lacking the mushroom perspective, I'll recall a different kind of illusion. When I saw Titian's painting *The Flaying of Marsyas* at an exhibition in London in the 1980s, I was overwhelmed by the work. I sat before the canvas for a very long time, awestruck by the savagery of the scene. I thought I could hear Apollo playing his violin and hear poor Marsyas moan; I know that I couldn't really hear these things, but my imagination conjured the sound of Apollo's fiddle. Other artwork has had a similar effect, but the Titian painting has stayed with me for thirty years. Mine was a very personal experience, though other art lovers have probably felt similar things in front of this magnificent work. But having enjoyed the intellectual clarity of an education a couple of millennia after Aristotle, I have no illusions whatsoever that my personal responses to art, or to anything else, reveal anything about the nature of the universe that is of any general consequence. In the same vein, the perceptions altered by mushroom toxins offer no possible revelations about the workings of the universe. Fortunately, there is a far more reliable way of learning things of wider application: this is called science.

It is important to appreciate, and for me to recognize here, that there are plenty of magic mushroomers who enjoy the occasional handful of psilocybes without encouraging any high-flown claims about the wider significance of the experience. But a handful of vocal advocates of magic mushrooming have done considerable harm to the study of mycology since the 1960s, adding a layer of silliness upon centuries of superstition and association with fairy tales. This is why the statement, "I have spent thirty years experimenting with fungi" sounds like a declaration of lunacy rather than one of sensible professional engagement. (By contrast, "I have spent the last thirty years experimenting with fruit flies" seems uncontroversial, doesn't it?) Following the ludicrous anthropological forays by Gordon Wasson, any hopes of an objective analysis of the clinical value of hallucinogenic mushrooms were sidelined by the narcissism of Timothy Leary and colleagues in the 1970s. But interest in this field was kept alive by a small number of investigators and at last, some important discoveries about the therapeutic value of psilocybes have emerged.

Psychiatrists and neuroscientists were very excited by a placebo-controlled study of the psychological effects of psilocybin on thirty volunteers in 2006.[18] Responses to this research, published in *Psychopharmacology*, were unusually effusive, with an editorial introducing the work and a series of expert commentaries published in the same issue of the journal. The study, led by Roland Griffiths, from the Johns Hopkins University School of Medicine, was exceptional both for its findings and because the investigators had been so careful in designing their experiments. The volunteers had responded to flyers publicizing a study of "a naturally occurring psychoactive substance" and were then screened by the researchers. Their response to the flyers meant that the test subjects had some level of interest in psychoactive substances, but none had histories of using magic mushrooms, nor suffered from any psychiatric disorders. Half of the group attended a church or synagogue, or were members of a meditation class, and all of them had participated in some kind of spiritual activities in the months before the study. This is significant, because it means that they were more likely to report some kind of spiritual experience than hardcore rationalists. Nevertheless, the results of the study were fascinating.

In a series of sessions, the participants were given a dose of purified psilocybin or placebo. After a few minutes, the psilocybin subjects became less responsive to questions posed by their monitors and went on to experience profound emotional changes, with some people crying, others feeling anxious, and many experiencing peace, harmony, and intense happiness. They sensed mood swings and changes in perception, and many of the participants reported that they felt the "unity of all things," the same "symptom" described by so many shroomers. An independent study in Europe reported similar symptoms among volunteers given very modest doses of psilocybin: they experienced "depersonalization," "loosening of ego boundaries," and a disrupted sense of time.[19] They also lost control of the rate at which they tapped their fingers in response to instructions from the investigators. This subtle motor dysfunction was clear when they were trying to tap at time intervals greater than two to three seconds, but not when they were told to tap at their maximum rate (try both tasks for yourself and you'll feel the difference immediately). This reflects psilocybin's stimulation of serotonin receptors and the importance of these membrane-embedded proteins in tasks that require voluntary commands. None of this would surprise a recreational shroomer, but the careful analysis in this study was necessary to identify the common threads of the psilocybin experience in the personal reflections of "hobbyists" posted on the Internet. The real surprises, at least for nonshroomers, came after the psilocybin sessions, when two-thirds of the volunteers at Johns Hopkins rated their experience as "either the single most meaningful experience" in their lives or "among the top five most meaningful experiences." They compared the significance of the experiment with the birth of a child or the death of a parent. Most of the group said that their reactions during the study had increased their sense of "personal well being or life satisfaction." The participants continued to report this sense of happiness more than a year after their psilocybin sessions.[20]

The Johns Hopkins study was the first attempt at an objective examination of hallucinogenic drugs in more than 40 years. The fact that exploration of the therapeutic value of psilocybin had been on hold for so long adds to the excitement of the new work. There are all kinds of prospects now for clinical studies to determine whether psilocybin or its derivatives might be used to combat depression, treat behavioral abnormalities and cluster headaches, and even to smooth one's passage to the grave. The idea that psilocybin might be useful in reducing the fear of death is encouraged by experiments in the 1970s, in which patients with terminal illnesses felt less anxious and fearful when treated with LSD. LSD, or lysergic acid diethyl-amide, is a semi-synthetic drug produced from lysergic acid, which, like psilocybin, is a fungal invention.[21] LSD shares a number of pharmacological properties with psilocybin and binds to the serotonin receptors favored by psilocin.

In the follow-up studies of the patients treated with psilocybin, many people described feeling closer to God.[22] Here's one of the comments published in the 2008 paper: "My conversation with God (golden streams of light) assur[ed] me that everything on this plane is perfect; but I do not have the physical body/mind to fully understand." And another: "The experience of death, which initially was very uncomfortable, followed by absolute peace and being in the presence of God. It was so awesome to be with God that words can't describe the experience." Remember that the participants were a spiritual group at the outset. It would be interesting to see the results of a future study comprising atheists and others lacking in spirituality like myself, but I am confident in the outcome. The rationalists would report all manner of emotional experiences—some lovely, some frightening—but I'm sure they wouldn't respond by saying that magic mushrooms had shown them their errors in thinking and that God had been there all the time, lurking in the wings, waiting for a chance to show them how everything works as soon as they got some psilocybin down their gullets. The only truth about God, or gods, revealed by taking psilocybin is that spiritual experiences are fully explainable in neuropharmacological terms.

The reason that some mushrooms produce chemicals that agitate our nervous systems is as murky as the reason that others produce toxins that can destroy our liver and kidneys. The quantity of psilocybin varies greatly among species of hallucinogenic mushrooms and may account for up to 1% or more of the weight of dried fruit bodies. Given that most of the dry weight of a mushroom is in cell wall materials, the amount of psilocybin is impressive. Levels of psilocybin are often much lower, but a "recommended" dosage of 5 grams of mushrooms provides the same kind of psilocybin hit that the Johns Hopkins researchers administered in purified form. The presence of this much of the drug in a handful of wild mushrooms certainly suggests that it does something useful for the fungus.

One obvious idea is that psilocybin serves as an antifeedant, discouraging insects and other animals from destroying spore-producing tissues. This is the idea I discussed in the previous chapter and is the most logical explanation for the evolution of mushroom toxins like alpha-amanitin. There haven't been any critical experiments to test the antifeedant hypothesis for psilocybin, but there has been some nice work demonstrating the insecticidal properties of the hallucinogens in fly agarics. Japanese researchers have shown that the development of fruit-eating flies is severely disrupted by exposure to ibotenic acid and muscimol, with fewer and fewer pupae surviving with increasing doses of the compounds. Ibotenic acid is much more potent than muscimol.[23] Irreflective of their common name, some *Drosophila* species eschew fruit in favor of a specialized diet of mushrooms. Experiments demonstrate that these insects are highly tolerant of both alkaloids, suggesting that they have evolved defense mechanisms to counteract the toxins synthesized by their prey. The insecticide hypothesis is encouraged by some of the common names for *Amanita muscaria*. The French, for example, call the fly agaric, "*une amanite tue-mouche*," the fly killer, and there is an ancient tradition of using pieces of fruit body to repel flies.[24] This may be a misreading of earlier names for the fungus, and of the simple "fly agaric" preferred by the British. An alternative idea is that the association between the mushroom and flies developed from the early interpretation of the mushroom's hallucinogenic properties as a form of demonic possession.[25] The link between flies and demons seems a bit tenuous, but it may (or may not) be worth considering that Beelzebub, the Hebrew name used as an alternate for Lucifer in Christianity, means "Lord of the Flies" in English. Early experiences with the hallucinogenic effects of the mushroom may also be reflected in the depiction of the tree of knowledge as a branched *Amanita* in a famous medieval fresco in the chapel of Plaincourault Abbey in central France. The fly agaric is a dangerous thing: "But the fruit of the tree which is in the midst of the garden, God hath said, ye shall not eat of it, neither shall ye touch it, lest you die." But it is also a temptation offered by the Devil: "And the serpent said unto the woman, ye shall not surely die. For God doth know that in the day ye eat thereof, then your eyes shall be opened, and ye shall be as gods, knowing good and evil." It's easy to see why so many shroomers have become enamored with the idea, voiced by John Allegro in 1970, that Christianity evolved from a mushroom-worshipping cult.[26] This isn't taken seriously today, but the French fresco certainly suggests that the fly agaric was manipulated as a religious symbol by some Christians in the thirteenth century.

Etymology aside, this discursion leaves us with the antifeedant model as the most likely explanation for the natural synthesis of hallucinogens. If psilocybin evolved as an antifeedant, it has had the opposite effect upon humans, attracting a sizeable population of pickers to the meadows where psilocybes thrive. Ibotenic acid and muscimol have failed the fly agaric for similar reasons, as I said in the previous chapter. On the plus side for psilocybes, there are plenty of people who love cultivating them in their basements, ensuring their conservation, like pigs raised for their bacon and chickens for their eggs.

Federal law in the United States doesn't identify magic mushrooms themselves as illegal drugs, but psilocybin and psilocin are listed, along with heroin and LSD, as Schedule I substances. This means that the possession of mushrooms is illegal if they contain the hallucinogens. Magic-mushroom spawn, which can be used to start a mushroom bed, is also illegal. Trade in the spores of magic mushrooms is seen as a legal loophole by some growers, because psilocybin hasn't been detected in the spores, but the business is a risky venture for everyone involved. In the United Kingdom, for example, mushroom possession can be punished by up to seven years in jail; supplying someone else with magic mushrooms can result in life imprisonment. Despite the tightening of restrictions, the business of mushroom growing seems to be thriving, based on the availability of shrooms sold in little plastic bags—there are, I presume, job opportunities for small-scale growers on both sides of the Atlantic. One of the factors limiting the market for shrooms is the fear expressed by potential users of "flashbacks," the possibility of frightening hallucinations that can return long after the mushrooms have been digested. This seems to be a very rare experience for shroomers, but it has a name in the medical literature—hallucinogen persisting perception disorder (HPPD)—and the small number of case studies are very nasty.[27] Aside from flashbacks, I am struck by research by neuropharmacologists concluding that psilocybin "induces a model psychosis which mimics certain aspects of acute and incipient stages of schizophrenia."[28] Stick to spring flowers and fine wines, that's my advice.

The sense of a deeper relationship with nature that is mentioned so often by people who have eaten magic mushrooms is difficult to explain based on our current understanding of cognition. This symptom of changing electrical activity in the neocortex hasn't been tied down to specific groups of neurons, but it will be, someday, if researchers employ high-resolution brain scanners to examine the effects of psilocybin and other hallucinogens. Unfortunately, however, the editorial in *Psychopharmacology* on the Johns Hopkins' research, written by Harriet de Wit, holds the door open to the influence of "ultimate realities that lie outside the purview of science."[29] This seems dangerous to me, inviting a return to pseudoscience after groundbreaking work.

Paul Stamets makes the case that the mushroom trips taken in the 1960s and '70s are linked to the birth of various social movements described under the umbrella of environmental activism. The common depersonalization experience of the psychonaut may be part of this, and if it takes a mushroom to redirect humanity toward a less destructive relationship with the rest of nature, then perhaps it's time to embrace mushroom worship on a global scale. After all, most versions of the God delusion seem hell-bent on negating our kinship with other living organisms and defiling the biosphere.

Speaking of God, the research on magic mushrooms could furnish humanity with the final nail in His coffin lid. If psilocybin can reproduce the symptoms of the religious experience of sudden closeness to God, the simplest interpretation is that this all-loving, ill-defined thing, the phantom presence that saved Timmy when he fell down the well (or was that Lassie?), and so on, is the product of our imagination. Gordon Wasson was right that mushrooms held the secret to understanding the origins of religion, but he was right for the wrong reason. His thesis, extended by followers, that modern religions evolved from ancient practices involving ritual inebriation with magic mushrooms is found wanting. But psilocybin is granting researchers access to a fresh and unambiguous neurological and cognitive explanation of the supernatural. The truth revealed is that faith in the supernatural has no more substance than a mushroom dream.

Chapter 8

Cures for Mortality?

THE MEDICINAL MUSHROOM FRAUD

This book is a celebration of a familiar, yet woefully underappreciated, part of nature, of the biology of parasol-shaped fruit bodies hooked into the roots of forest trees, brackets that burgeon from decaying logs, phallic eruptions from garden beds, gigantic puffballs, and white buttons in the grocery store: masterpieces of bioengineering. It is also a plea for rationality in exploring this subject, because mycology, unlike other subjects of scientific inquiry, has been ravaged by centuries of superstition. Folklore attending mushrooms has helped keep them in the human consciousness, but it has also made them the focus of illogic. The backwaters of mycology are a hiding place for the uneducated, where people are shameless in their revelry in ill-formulated ideas about supernatural forces.

The association between mushrooms and witches in dark forests, et cetera, might have withered in the last century but for the popularity, beginning in the 1960s, of hallucinogenic species. The culture of shrooming, coupled with European mythology, resulted in the unedited love of all things mushroom for the most enthusiastic disciples. Today, this countercultural phenomenon (for lack of a crisper label) is responsible for encouraging the irrational belief that something as strange as a mushroom *must* have mystical powers and *might*, therefore, hold the key to stimulating an aging immune system, rebooting a flagging sex life, purifying internal organs poisoned by modern life, and even keeping a dying patient alive. This chapter concludes this book's appeal for the appreciation of one of nature's greatest products unencumbered by groundless guesswork, wishful thinking, and commercial exploitation camouflaged by the conceit of spiritual superiority.

My dear father, Roy, died in 2009, having developed pleural mesothelioma, the asbestos cancer, without any memorable exposure to the reputed cause. He survived for longer than many patients following diagnosis and enjoyed a year of relative well-being after chemotherapy, whose side effects were bearable only because they ceased, eventually, after each treatment. A few months after his death, I read the following statement by Mike Adams, the editor of an online newsletter, NaturalNews.com:

> The cure for cancer already exists. But it wasn't created in a lab, and it wasn't funded by pink-ribbon products or walkathons. It was created for free by Mother Nature, and it exists as a collection of literally thousands of powerful anti-cancer phytonutrients found in medicinal mushrooms.[1]

If only I had known: Dad's illness could have been treated with capsules of dried mushrooms! He would still be alive today, because "*The cure for cancer already exists.*" And the news keeps getting better—the benefits of mushrooms extend well beyond the aspirations of the cancer patient. Indeed, contrary to the international conspiracy of the modern medical profession to enslave the populations of wealthy developed countries to the pharmaceutical industry—"Big Pharma"—mushrooms offer low-cost deliverance from all manner of illnesses. Read this posting from www.botanicalpreservationcorps. com:

Medicinal mushrooms may possess the solutions to many maladies plaguing modern man. Science has found a multitude of beneficent active compounds, with the greatest focus on immunopotentiating complex sugar molecules known as polysaccharides, unique to each species.[2]

Botanical Preservation Corps, an organization based in Sebastopol, California, is "Dedicated to furthering human relations with the harmonious resonant constituents of the botanical realm." (The words "beneficent" and "harmonious" should serve as a warning to all skeptics searching for objective medical information.) A dozen different extracts are sold through its website, including *Polyporus umbellatus*:

Contemporary scientific research reveals it to be strongly anti-tumor, a natural antibiotic, antimalarial, antiinflammatory and liver protective. Chinese studies have found it significantly effective in treating cirrhosis, hepatitis B and in aiding the immune system of patients in recovery from lung cancer chemotherapy.

Similarly fantastic claims are made about a dozen or more mushrooms, but I want to begin by looking more closely at *Polyporus umbellatus*. Colonies of this fungus invade the roots of hardwood trees, causing white rot, and forms massive clusters of trumpet-shaped mushrooms whose stalks can become fused into a solid mass at their bases. In addition to the mushrooms, this species produces sclerotia, underground concretions of hyphae from which the colony can expand or fresh mushrooms can sprout. Sclerotia of some fungi are rounded, but this *Polyporus* creates a branched structure with a wrinkled, blackened surface. They look like the dried turds of a moose or any similar-sized ungulate suffering from irritable bowel syndrome. These have been used in traditional Chinese medicine for their diuretic effects. The sclerotia are inserted, inch by inch, into the rectum of the patient, until they compress the bladder and induce copious urination. That's not entirely true, not true at all really, though the suppositorial dosage would be in lockstep with the kind of silliness that informed a great deal of ancient and largely ineffective medicine. The authentic application of the fungus involves the use of shavings of the sclerotia, known as Zhu-Ling, to prepare an herbal tea. I have no doubt whatsoever that a cup of this will make the tiniest grandmother piss like a racehorse. My suspicions grow, however, when the accessory powers of this elixir are considered.

Purveyors of Zhu-Ling in the United States suggest that its usefulness goes way beyond its traditional prescription as a diuretic. On the website for Fungi Perfecti (Paul Stamets' company, discussed in Chapter 7), it is listed for its anti-bacterial, anti-inflammatory, anti-tumor, and anti-viral effects; for its effects on the immune system; as a liver tonic; and for its efficacy in treating respiratory problems.[3] There is *some* scientific basis for *some* of these claims.[4] Zhu-Ling extracts injected into the peritoneum of mice inhibited the rate of tumor growth; extracts also killed different kinds of cancer cells grown in culture flasks and reduced the recurrence of cancer in patients after surgery for carcinoma of the bladder. This is just the beginning. Extracts from the mushroom have stimulatory effects upon the immune system, promote hair growth in humans, are effective in treating chlamydial infections, and are effective as anti-malarial agents.[5] The problem with the science behind these claims is that they are of uncertain reliability: most were published in Chinese journals in the 1980s, and it is very difficult (probably impossible) to determine the quality of the original research. This does not mean that extracts from this bracket fungus lack benefits in treating certain types of cancer, but it certainly demands a lot of careful investigation before we proclaim that it is a cure for cancer.

Unlike many other mushrooms, *Polyporus umbellatus* is not celebrated for its hypotensive effects, nor for its properties in stabilizing blood sugar, nor for reducing cholesterol, nor for providing one with erections admirable both for their strength and their duration. One cannot expect to get everything from a single mushroom species, which is why mycomerchants promote the sale of mixtures of extracts from multiple kinds of mushroom. Fungi Perfecti sells capsules that contain substances from "17 powerful mushrooms." These must be particularly useful for diabetic patients with recurrent bladder cancer who continue to enjoy a vigorous sex life in the rare moments when they are not washing down handfuls of mushroom capsules with Turkey Tail Mushroom Tea, using their MycoShield™ Throat Spray, enjoying a full-body massage with a gel fortified with a bracket fungus, and feeding their pets with MUSH™ Mushroom Blend for Pets, which has been "taste-tested and approved by dogs, cats and horses." Almost every member of the household is covered for every ailment, and I'm sure that someone would recommend a mushroom extract for your scrofulous hamster if you were to ask.

The disclaimer at the bottom of the Botanical Preservation Corps web page is a standard feature for the industry, but it is, of course, at odds with the entire enterprise: "The statements on our website are not intended as medical advice and have not been evaluated by the FDA. Our products are not intended to diagnose, treat, cure or prevent any disease. This notice is required by the federal "food, drug & cosmetic act." Fungi Perfecti goes with a simpler version: "These statements have not been evaluated by the Food and Drug Administration." The devil is in this fine print.

The U.S. Food and Drug Administration (FDA) is charged with protecting the public by ensuring the safety of drugs and medical devices, our food supply, cosmetics, dietary supplements, medical imaging equipment and other "radiation-emitting" products. A patent waste of public dollars, according to the most foaming-at-mouth libertarians; a useful arm of government for the rest of us who do not trust companies to eliminate mercury from medicines, ensure that "salad" and "hepatitis" do not become synonyms, and check that one's next dental X-ray does not result in singed hair, blackened lips, and tooth loss. Like other dietary supplements, mushrooms sold as medicines are regulated as foods rather than medicines, which means that they can be marketed as treatments for everything from sagging skin to lung cancer without FDA approval.[6] The FDA has control over manufacturing practices, ensuring that mushroom capsules are free from fecal contamination and so on, and it also has jurisdiction over labeling. This explains the provisos printed on mushroom products. Once the lack of FDA approval is stated, companies have considerable latitude in advertising the potency of their products. Fungi Perfecti is not alone in the boldness of its claims, but I'll pick a few items from its catalog: a blend of seven mushrooms is described as a "tonic" (a category of limitless vacuity) "for maintaining peak performance and health"; capsules containing extracts from a single species are sold as a source of "health-enhancing, anti-inflammatory and anti-oxidant properties"; and "homeopathic topical soothing lotion" is recommended for treating "soft tissue ailments" including "carpal tunnel syndrome and other compression neuropathies."[7] The active ingredient in the lotion is the bracket fungus, *Fomitopsis officinalis*, which offers "a safe, natural way to stimulate the body to heal the damage that causes pain." It is possible that these claims are true, but they are not based on any clinical evidence.

The Federal Trade Commission (FTC) is a second independent government agency concerned about bogus claims made on behalf of mushrooms. Foremost among the FTC's recommendations to consumers is that they ask their physicians for advice about medicinal supplements. This seems indubitably prudent advice; the supplement industry is unlikely to go beyond printing disclaimers in very small print on its labels unless it is forced to do so. Increasing oversight by two powerful agencies of the United States government is a direct threat to the profitability of the medicinal mushroom market, fueling a cat-and-mouse game between mushroom suppliers making "cancer-cure" claims and the federal government sending threatening letters. Efforts to settle this impasse through legislation are unlikely to result in an immediate fix, but perhaps things are moving in the right direction for consumers.[8]

Policies on supplements in the European Union are broadly similar to those in the United States, and the essential concerns for consumer protection are the same. In the end, everything must rest upon the scientific evidence for the efficacy of mushroom extracts at treating illnesses. And (said the author with pitiful naiveté) the corporate lobbyist is not going to be the ultimate arbiter in any democratic country; study after study finds wide public support for greater government oversight of the health claims on supplement labels.[9] People want to know what pills they are swallowing and whether they have any prospect of shrinking their boils.

To this end, there have been a few recent studies that seek an objective evaluation of the pharmacological effects of mushrooms. There is evidence that the polysaccharides that form much of the wall material that surrounds fungal cells may affect the growth of tumors. These strings of sugar molecules are called beta-glucans, and there are several kinds of them defined by the position of the chemical linkages between the sugars. The glucans can form long spirals, or single helices, and can intertwine to form more complicated structures called triple helices. These strands are threaded about one another and with other molecules, including chitin, to create the tough weft of wall material that protects the watery cytoplasm of the cells. The glucans can be extracted from mushroom tissue by boiling in water, or dissolving with alkali or ethanol, or they can be purified by digesting surrounding materials with enzymes. The effects of the purified glucans are tested by mixing them with various preparations of blood cells or by injecting them into mice. The results of these experiments, while promising, are not as straightforward as Beth Ley, Ph.D., proclaims in her booklet, *Discover the Beta Glucan Secret*: "Beta glucan triggers an immune response in the body creating a system of defense against viral, bacterial, fungal, parasitic or potentially cancerous invaders."[10]

Mushroom glucans have been shown to enhance the activity of dendritic cells, which play crucial roles in our immune defenses, including the recognition of cancer cells. (Immunology 101: Dendritic cells process antigens and present them to T cells; T cells are modified into helper T cells, and helper T cells produce interferon and interleukins and induce other players in the immune system including macrophages, eosinophils, and B cells that produce antibodies.) Most of the evidence of interactions between glucans and dendritic cells are seen in "test-tube" experiments, but related responses have also been shown in mice.[11] Most important, mice injected with glucans show varying degrees of protection against tumor growth: some researchers suggest that glucan injections act like a vaccine against tumors. Mice injected with glucans also show enhanced macrophage function, and mice fed with mushroom glucans show increased activity of another cell type in the immune system, the natural killer cell. These results are based upon a number of articles published in peer-reviewed journals, but the work on animals is very limited and impaired by poor experimental design. The authors of a major review on the immunobiology of mushrooms concluded that "the research is not systematic."[12]

Another group of researchers from MD Anderson Cancer Center, in Houston, Texas, conducted a detailed review of the studies on a single medicinal mushroom, *Trametes versicolor*.[13] This mushroom, whose common name is turkey tail, was mentioned in Chapter 3: it causes white rot, forms fused clusters of thin brackets whose upper surfaces are colored in concentric stripes, and is one of the least exciting fungi to look at. There has been interest in the potential anti-tumor properties of this mushroom for decades, and a particular cell wall component called polysaccharide K (or PSK) has shown promise in mice studies. PSK is a type of proteoglycan, a polysaccharide bonded to a protein, and its mechanism of action is different from the immune stimulation caused by beta-glucans. Some researchers suggest that PSK acts as an antioxidant and that it has a protective effect against chromosome damage. The compound has also been associated with direct inhibition of tumor-cell development. A second molecule extracted from turkey tail, called PSP, also shows anti-tumor properties in mice experiments. PSP has a variety of effects upon the immune system, but, as with PSK, it is its antioxidant properties that have attracted the most interest. The investigators at MD Anderson carried out an exhaustive review of the published work on these compounds. Studies in Asia have compared the survival of patients diagnosed with colorectal cancer treated with standard chemotherapy plus oral PSK, with patients treated with chemotherapy alone. Survival rates after ten years were higher for the PSK patients. Similar conclusions have been reached in studies of patients suffering from lung cancer. The majority of the human studies on PSK and PSP included a control group of patients that did not receive the mushroom extracts, but only one of forty studies published between 1997 and 2005 met the hallmark of a randomized controlled and blinded clinical trial. In common with the glucan studies, the research on *Trametes versicolor* extracts is full of holes, but the results are provocative. It is *possible* that further research will lead to novel cancer therapies. This sentence is unambiguous and bears no relation to the outrageous claims made by mushroom merchants about their products.

Among the mushrooms sold as medicinals, reishi and shiitake are probably best known. Reishi is the Japanese name for the bracket fungus, *Ganoderma lucidum*, which has been used as a remedy for a multitude of ailments, ranging from constipation to cancer, for thousands of years in Asia. It is also called the mushroom of immortality. Its fruit bodies have a distinctive glossy or varnished finish with a striking reddish-brown color. Michael Kuo, editor of mushroomexpert.com, calls it "one of the most beautiful mushrooms in the world." It is related to the monstrous *Ganoderma applanatum*, artist's conk, celebrated in Chapter 2 for its trillion-spore output, but *Ganoderma lucidum* can get very big indeed and probably comes close to matching the conk's fecundity (Plate 16).[14] Its mycelium rots hardwood, sometimes attacking living trees and otherwise decomposing fallen timber. It is cultivated on shaded or buried logs in China and Japan and harvested for up to five years after it begins to fruit. They are also grown in a "rapid cycle system" from bags of woodchips and sawdust that have been soaked in molasses.[15] Fruiting begins from stacks of the culture bags in a month or so. There has been a lot of animal research on the effects of extracts from the hardened fruit bodies along much the same lines as the investigations on *Trametes* and other medicinal mushrooms. Human clinical studies are also plentiful and emphasize the beneficial effects of reishi on lung and

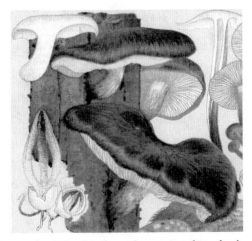

Figure 8.1. *Lentinula edodes*, shiitake, with a species of *Pseudocolus*, a stinkhorn, shown lower left.
Source: From S. Kawamura, *Illustrations of Japanese Fungi* (Tokyo: The Bureau of Forestry, 1911–1925).

heart function. Again, little of the work is published in English, and almost none of it meets the kind of rigorous criteria required of prescription medicines.

The gilled mushroom *Lentinula edodes*, shiitake, is the best-known medicinal mushroom (Fig. 8.1). It has been cultivated for a millennium or more, and claims for its powers are quite similar to those made for other mushrooms, only more plentiful in print and online. The following comment on www.shiitakemushroomlog.com is typical:

Shiitakes...have natural antiviral and immunity-boosting properties and are used nutritionally to fight viruses, lower cholesterol and regulate blood pressure. Lentinan, an immunostimulant derived from shiitakes, has been used to treat cancer, AIDS, diabetes, chronic fatigue syndrome, fibrocystic breast disease, and other conditions with impressive results.

The purportedly active compounds in shiitake include its version of cell-wall beta-glucan, called lentinan, and a polysaccharide-protein hybrid extracted from its mycelium abbreviated as LEM. In his book, *Medicinal Mushrooms*, Christopher Hobbs, L. Ac. (licensed acupuncturist), says, "Shiitake is used medicinally for any and all diseases including depressed immune function, including cancer, AIDS, Candida infections…and frequent flu and colds."[16] The AIDS claim is interesting, isn't it? A modern scourge of humanity, an incurable viral illness whose management using antiretroviral drugs is a triumph of modern medicine and the pharmaceutical research, now treatable with shiitake mushrooms! You will not be surprised to learn that this amazing assertion, widespread on the Internet, isn't based upon a substantial body of carefully designed clinical studies. You will be surprised to discover (I was flabbergasted) that the "evidence" derives from a single study of two patients, at least one of whom was not HIV positive, that was published in 1984. The most compelling thing about the work is that it appeared in a highly regarded periodical, *The Lancet*, and was authored by an international group of scientists from premier institutions in Japan, France, and the United States.[17] The publication of the study in 1984 is crucial: the disease didn't have a name until 1982, and the cause was unknown until the virus was isolated from a single patient at the Pasteur Institute in 1983. One of the patients in the shiitake study was recovering from breast cancer therapy, had a low white cell count, and antibodies to the viruses HTLV I and III in her blood serum. (HTLV III was the name used for the AIDS virus until HIV was coined in 1986.) It is possible that she was exposed to the virus through a blood transfusion. After this patient received lentinan via an intravenous drip, her lymphocyte and platelet counts rebounded, the activity of her natural killer cells was restored, and subsequent blood tests failed to detect either virus. Similar results were seen in the second patient, but he tested positive only for HTLV I, a virus that causes T-cell leukemia and T-cell lymphoma but that isn't associated with AIDS at all.

Given the timing of the study, the investigators can be excused for their zeal, but the misuse of their findings in the twenty-first century is immoral. There is no evidence whatsoever that lentinan is an effective therapy for individuals dealing with the immune damage that terminates in AIDS. I feel livid as I write, considering the helplessness of the patient who stumbles upon the website for ABO Switzerland Company, for example, which offers a two-page listing of "Natural Anti-HIV" products, including lentinan, reishi mushroom extract, "Colla Corii Asini (Donkey-hide Glue)," and turtle shell extract.[18]

The preposterous claims made for lentinan overshadow its demonstrable biological activity and effects upon the immune system. The marketers of shiitake products assume that the allure of their merchandise grows with the adornment of fantastical cancer-cure claims. This may backfire. When I venture into a drugstore looking for something to soothe an insect bite, I would not grab for the ointment that promised, in addition to its anti-inflammatory properties, a cure for arthritis or syphilis. While I do not suffer from arthritis, nor harbor spirochetes, my confidence in the sting ointment would be diminished greatly by its reported lack of specificity. The absence of statements about the side effects of medicinal mushrooms also says a lot about the paucity of science behind the product claims. Anything with the powerful pharmacological properties claimed for mushroom extracts would surely come with an array of debilitating side effects. The absence of side effects points to an absence of medicinal utility. If future research demonstrates that lentinan is a useful pharmaceutical product, its acceptance in the marketplace may be marred by today's catholic, cure-all marketing strategy. Remembering the hype from earlier decades, wary consumers in 2025 may think "snake-oil" when they watch the holographic advertisements in the iPaper. This should be considered by anyone who is serious about developing a long-term market for medicinal mushrooms.

The mix of shiitake cell-wall glucans labeled as lentinan does have a stimulatory effect upon a number of players in the immune system. But nobody has established whether these ropy molecules from shiitake have a stronger effect upon the immune response of an experimental animal than do glucans from any other mushroom. The fact that lentinan rouses lymphocytes is not, in itself, at all surprising. Animals and fungi have shared the planet since their split from some single-celled ancestor more than a billion years ago, and the fungi have probably been infecting animals for much of that time. The Atlantic horseshoe crab, *Limulus polyphemus*, derives from an Ordovician lineage of spider relatives. The crab's immune system is quite simple, with a single type of cell, called an amebocyte. Amebocytes recognize bacteria in the crab's bloodstream and induce a coagulation reaction that forms an immobilizing gel around the invading cells. Fungal glucans cause the same reaction.[19] The fact that the horseshoe crab's simple immune system responds to little else but bacteria and fungi illustrates the overriding threat posed to animals by these microorganisms. In light of the crab's sensitivity to glucans, it is not at all surprising that lentinan upsets the much more complicated immune system of humans. It is also useful to consider whether it is a good thing to stimulate one's immune system. If the immune response to viruses is impaired, then a stronger response would be a good thing. If the immune response results in inflammation, we might reconsider the benefits of deliberate stimulation: what is the advantage of boosting the cellular mechanisms that result in eczema, hives, hay fever, asthma, food allergies, and life-threatening anaphylactic reactions? Might immune stimulation exacerbate autoimmune diseases and even promote the spread of cancer cells? "Rather than 'boosting' the immune system," wrote Harriet Hall, for *Skeptic Magazine,* "we should try to keep it functioning normally."[20] Yet facts are of no significance when the consumer is sufficiently gullible.

Which brings me to Dr. Andrew Weil, founder and program director of the Arizona Center for Integrative Medicine in Tucson and monarch of an empire of alternative medical services and products. His commercial interests in mushrooms are limited to a single product line, but he deserves some extra scrutiny here because his view of medicine reflects so many of the limitations and the excesses of the medicinal-mushroom business. Weil has a generous beard and twinkly eyes, and he has prospered as a proponent of the healing powers of plants, mushrooms, and "higher consciousness." He is the author of numerous bestselling books on alternative medicine, beginning with *The Natural Mind,* published in the 1970s,[21] and has trademarked his self-proclaimed title as "Your Trusted Health Advisor," dispensing advice on healthy aging, vitamins, supplements, and "balanced living." Unlike most of his competitors in the field of alternative medicine, Weil boasts an Ivy League medical degree and "considers himself an authority on almost every field of medicine."[22] He has been very successful in cultivating the image of a tremendously contented, self-satisfied, and contemplative health guru and has boosted sales of his books and medicinals by appearances as a regular guest on television talk shows. Recognizing the limited tolerance for narcotics expressed by a good chunk of the more mature and medically needy population of the United States, Weil has sought to distance himself from his earlier enthusiasm for mind-altering drugs—though he says that he was cured of his allergy to feline dander by letting a cat sit on his lap during an LSD trip[23]—claiming the role of a sage in the current national effort to reform health care. In recent years he has written much more on healthy diets than on the therapeutic value of recreational drugs, wishful thinking, meditation, and so on. I wonder, based on his efforts to be taken seriously as a health care professional, whether he regrets that a new species of hallucinogenic mushroom was named after him in the 1990s: *Psilocybe weilii* smells like a cucumber and grows only in northern Georgia.[24]

The introduction of fungi into cosmetic products increases their cost, transforms a face cream into a cosmeceutical, and often results in vigorous sales. The term "cosmeceutical" applies to anything that might be called a cosmetic that contains ingredients that the producers suggest have some kind of medical benefit. In other words, the term is absent of any clear meaning but implies, for example, that massaging an odorous paste into your sun-damaged skin may be good for you. Weil promotes a host of these kinds of products through his Origins line (Dr. Andrew Weil[TM] for Origins), including "Weil Juvenon," a "science-based supplement" that helps "protect and maintain healthy cells," and a "total integrative approach to skin care."[25] Weil uses a "Mega-Mushroom blend" in his face cream and cleanser, eye makeup remover, "eye serum," lip balm, body cream, "bedtime balm," and more besides. These cosmetics contain multiple ingredients, but the website doesn't make clear pronouncements about the activity of the Mega-Mushroom blend beyond general statements about moisturizing and protection from oxidation. While there is no evidence whatsoever that mushrooms confer any benefits as additives in cosmetics, they do add a whiff of exoticism to the petroleum gels that consumers, mostly women, slather on their faces.[26]

Mushrooms are used in numerous lines of skin care products and celebrated for their antioxidant properties. It is difficult to make unambiguous statements about mushroom antioxidants, because this takes us into a field of pseudoscience that is a domain of limitless obfuscation. Antioxidants are big business, and the term "powerful antioxidant" is stamped on all manner of products. Breakfast cereals have been marketed for their antioxidant effects and for their potency as immune boosters, although the FDA is working to stop these practices.

Living things, including us, are damaged by oxidation. All of our molecular constituents, from the lipids in our cell membranes to our proteins and genetic material, are susceptible to oxidative attack, and long-term damage at this submicroscopic scale can result in injury to tissues and organs. Chemicals that oxidize our molecules come from our environment and are also produced naturally through our metabolism. Our cells compensate by producing protective antioxidant molecules, including enzymes like catalase, superoxide dismutase, and peroxidases. There are many compounds in our foods that also act as antioxidants when they are tested in the lab, which is how we get from breakfast cereal to protecting one's children. The argument made by cereal manufacturers is that because their products contain antioxidants, they may be a beneficial part of our diet. The problem with this is that there is no evidence that antioxidants in the foods we eat act as protective antioxidants when we absorb them into our bodies.

Colorful fruits and vegetables are rich in antioxidants, and populations that eat diets rich in these foods tend to show lower rates of cancer and other plagues of modern life. This observation doesn't begin to make a causal linkage between dietary antioxidants and human health. Such a link may exist, but the science isn't there to support it. Other interpretations of the healthful effects of colorful foods include the high fiber content of fruits and vegetables, and the decreased reliance on processed foods in diets rich in unprocessed things. Mushrooms contain antioxidants, mostly in the form of phenolic compounds. These may be beneficial constituents, but they are not found in concentrations that exceed those found in many fruits and vegetables and don't come close to the levels measured in cranberries. The link between dietary antioxidants and our health is unclear; the link between antioxidants in face creams and skin rejuvenation is nonexistent.

As you have gathered, mine is a negative view of the medicinal-mushroom industry. Productive skepticism requires an ever-open mind, however, and I am hopeful that pseudoscience will be replaced by real science in the continuing analysis of mushroom pharmacology. Some insiders express similar sentiments, feeling more positive about the existing studies, perhaps, while recognizing the need for proper clinical trials if the market for medicinal mushrooms is ever going to be aligned with the proven effects of existing prescription drugs.[27] Indeed, it would be irrational to view past blunders as a reason for abandoning the quest for novel therapeutic compounds. Natural-product chemists may open a limitless almanac of potentially useful compounds by expanding their purview from the small number of mushroom species that have been examined in any detail to consider the thousands, or tens of thousands, of obscure and nameless basidiomycetes. Some proportion of the molecules synthesized by mushrooms to attract or repel invertebrates will interact with human chemistry, and a small proportion of these molecules may prove beneficial in the treatment of disease. In addition to animal attractants and antifeedants, antibacterial compounds secreted by mushrooms and their colonies might be co-opted as future antibiotics for treating infections.

Consider a beautiful mushroom like the rooting shank, *Xerula furfuracea*, from a biochemical perspective: its broad beige cap is supported on a long, stiff stem above a buried knot of decaying roots at the base of a dying tree (Fig. 8.2); its woodland habitat is heaving with life, yet the mushroom continues to cast clouds of white spores from

Figure 8.2. *Xerula furfuracea*, rooting shank.
Source: From R. K. Greville, *Scottish Cryptogamic Flora*, vol. 4 (Edinburgh: Maclachlan and Stewart, 1826).

its thick white gills for a week, clean and undamaged by crawling animals that might profit from a burst of calories if only they could digest its flesh. The rooting shank, like every mushroom, exhibits chemical mastery over its neighborhood. Future drugs may be stuck in its cell walls, tethered to its membranes and diffusing through its chilly cytoplasm.[28] Mushrooms deserve a five-star rating for bioprospecting. For the time being, though, *caveat emptor*.

NOTES

Chapter 1

1. Recent papers on the subject of basidiospore dispersal: D.-W. Li, *Mycological Research* 109, 1235–1242 (2005); B. Nordén and K.-H. Larsson, *Nordic Journal of Botany* 20, 215–219 (2008); N. Hallenberg and N. Kúffer, *Nordic Journal of Botany* 21, 431–436 (2008).
2. R. W. Wilson and E. S. Beneke, *Mycologia* 58, 328–332 (1966).
3. E. Lax, *The Mold in Dr. Florey's Coat: The Story of the Penicillin Miracle* (New York: Henry Holt, 2004).
4. M. Malpighi, *Anatome Plantarum* (London: Johannis Martyn, 1675–1679).
5. P. A. Micheli, *Nova Plantarum Genera* (Florence: Bernardi Paperinii, 1729).
6. The significance of Prévost's work is described in N. P. Money, *The Triumph of the Fungi: A Rotten History* (New York: Oxford University Press, 2007), 103–108.
7. O. Brefeld, *Botanische Untersuchungen über Schimmelpilze* (Leipzig: A. Felix, 1872–1912).
8. Potter's paintings are reproduced in W. P. K. Findlay, *Wayside and Woodland Fungi* (London: Frederick Warne, 1967).
9. C. Schmitt and M. L. Tatum, *The Malheur National Forest. Location of the World's Largest Living Organism [The Humongous Fungus]* (USDA Forest Service, Pacific Northwest Division, 2008). The largest individual (colony) is estimated to weigh between 7,600 and 35,000 tons.
10. Here are some details. Dikaryons form when compatible monokaryons fuse, and compatibility is determined by a pair of mating-type genes, which are designated A and B. In some fungi, there are hundreds of different versions, or

alleles, of each mating factor. Incompatible reactions occur when monokary-ons that share one or both mating type alleles attempt to fuse: A1B1 x A1B1, A1B1 x A1B2, or A1B1 x A2B1 don't work. In an A1B1 x A2B2 cross, and hun-dreds or thousands of other crosses, however, a fully functioning dikaryon is produced, and this has the potential to generate a fertile fruit body. When a compatible reaction occurs, nuclei from both mating types migrate through one another's colonies, converting the monokaryon into a dikaryon. This pro-cess is termed dikaryotization.

11. A. de Bary, *Comparative Morphology and Taxonomy of the Fungi Mycetozoa and Bacteria*, English translation (Oxford: Clarendon Press, 1887).

12. L. R. Tulasne and C. Tulasne, *Selecta Fungorum Carpologia*, 3 vols., translated by W. B. Grove, edited by A. H. R. Buller and C. L. Shear (Oxford: Clarendon Press, 1931). Seek copies of the original volumes published in Paris between 1861 and 1865 for the breathtaking luminosity of the first printing of the illustrations.

13. W. G. Smith, *Grevillea* 4, 53–63 (1875); the quote is from p. 60.

14. W. G. Smith, *Journal of Botany* 2, 215–218 (1864); W. G. Smith, *Mushrooms and Toadstools: How to Distinguish Easily the Differences Between Edible and Poisonous Fungi: With Two Large Sheets Containing Figures of Twenty-nine Edible and Thirty-one Poisonous Species Drawn the Natural Size and Coloured from Living Specimens* (London: R. Hardwicke, 1867).

15. E. M. Wakefield, *Naturwissenschaften Zeitschrift für Forst- und Landwirtschaft* 7, 521–551 (1909).

16. D. Moore and A. Meškauskas, *Mycological Research* 110, 251–256 (2006).

17. J. W. Taylor and C. E. Ellison, *PNAS* 107, 11655–11656 (2010). Complex multi-cellularity may have evolved several times among the eukaryotes, with separate developmental mechanisms arising in the animals, plants, ascomycetes, and basidiomyctes.

18. A. Meškauskas, L. J. McNulty, and D. Moore, *Mycological Research* 108, 341–353 (2004); N. P. Money, *Nature* 431, 32 (2004).

19. D. Moore et al., *Mycological Research* 100, 257–273 (1996).

20. N. P. Money, *BioEssays* 24, 949–952 (2002).

21. The inflation of pre-existing hyphae appears to be sufficient to account for stem and cap expansion in some mushrooms, while the continuous proliferation of hyphal branches occurs during the development of other species. D. Moore, in *Patterns in Fungal Development*, edited by S.-W. Chiu and D. Moore (Cambridge: Cambridge University Press, 1996), 1–36.

22. N. P. Money and J. P. Ravishankar, *Mycological Research* 109, 627–634 (2005).

23. The tips of individual hyphae can apply maximum pressures of 1 or 2 atmo-spheres as they penetrate rotting wood or other food sources. Hyphae exert an average pressure of about two-thirds of an atmosphere when they are bundled into the stems of mushrooms, allowing the fruit body to push through soil and

emerge into the air. A dense patch of mushrooms growing from area of 0.01 m^2 exerting the average pressure produces a total force of 676 N. The strongest mushrooms can raise a snoozing reader plus brandy balloon plus cat with a combined mass of 73 kg and gravitational force of 715 N; the average mushroom patch cannot do so until the 4-kg cat jumps from the reader's lap, reducing the load by 39 N (to 676 N).

24. G. Straatsma, F. Ayer, and S. Egli, *Mycological Research* 105, 515–523 (2001).

25. Mr. Limbaugh continues to express this opinion on his radio show two decades after committing this to print in R. Limbaugh, *See, I Told You So* (New York: Pocket Books, 1993).

26. H. Kauserud et al., *PNAS* 105, 3811–3814 (2008).

Chapter 2

1. A. H. R. Buller, *Researches on Fungi*, vols. 1–6 (London: Longmans, Green, 1909–1934), vol. 7 (Toronto: Toronto University Press, 1950).

2. Like other brilliant observations by the Florentine naturalist, Micheli's quartets were ignored, and subsequent investigators illustrated a variety of spore-producing structures that have never existed in a gilled mushroom. In study after study, scientists who had made other valid observations about fungi illustrated spores within sacs that looked like asci. Asci are the squirt guns formed by fungi that belong to a related phylum called the Ascomycota. The investigators deluded themselves that these sacs that were ubiquitous among the ascomycetes *had* to occur in the basidiomycetes, too. This was a monumental act of self-deception, because the actual arrangement, with spores formed on the outside of their supporting basidia, is observed easily at a fairly low magnification. They saw what they expected to see. The mistake was uncovered by a handful of mycologists—or fungologists, as they might have referred to themselves—in the 1830s. August Corda, curator at the National Museum in Prague, may have been the first of the dissidents, but his illustrations of external spores were dismissed as those of insect eggs. Corda holds the distinction of being the only mycologist to have drowned after a shipwreck, his expiration occurring in the Caribbean following a collecting trip in Texas in 1849. The perspicacity of his microscopic observations is a counterpoint to his forecast that the city of Houston would "disintegrate just as quickly as it rose."

3. N. P. Money, *Mr. Bloomfield's Orchard: The Mysterious World of Mushrooms, Molds, and Mycologists* (New York: Oxford University Press, 2002).

4. In *Mr. Bloomfield's Orchard* (n. 3), p. 12, I made an error in scaling the speed of a mushroom spore to human dimensions. A human traveling 100 times his or her own length (height) in 1 millisecond would by flying at 612,000 kilometers per hour, or about 400,000 miles per hour, not the comparatively sedate 400 miles per hour stated in this earlier narrative.

5. The only organisms that show any similar mechanism of spore discharge are a group of slime molds called the protostelids, but the way that this process works in these protists isn't clear.

6. M. L. Berbee and J. W. Taylor, *Fungal Biology Reviews* 24, 1–16 (2010).

7. L. Yafetto, et al., *PLoS ONE* 3(9): e3237 doi:10.1371/journal.pone.0003237 (2008). Six phyla are recognized in the current taxonomic arrangement of the Kingdom Fungi: Basidiomycota (including the mushroom-forming species), Ascomycota, Glomeromycota, and aquatic fungi that produce swimming spores organized in the Blastocladiomycota, Chytridiomycota, and Neocallimastigomycota. Genetic data indicate that some fungi do not fit neatly within any of these groups, but we don't have sufficient information to delineate additional phyla. These "homeless" microorganisms include 900 or more species of zygomycete, including *Pilobolus*. In addition to these fungi, there are more than 1,000 species of animal parasite called microsporidia that some authorities regard as part of the kingdom.

8. C. T. Ingold, *Transactions of the British Mycological Society* 51, 592–594 (1968); C. T. Ingold, *Fungal Spores: Their Liberation and Dispersal* (Oxford: Clarendon Press, 1971); M. Roper et al., *PNAS* 105, 20583–20588 (2010).

9. The number of spores released by brackets of *Ganoderma* was estimated by Buller (n. 1).

10. J. Taggart, S. A. Hutchinson, and P. Swinbank, *Annals of Botany* 28, 607–618 (1964).

11. F. Darwin (ed.), *More Letters of Charles Darwin*, vol. 1 (London: John Murray, 1903); quotation from letter 97, March 21, 1860.

12. More details on mushroom cooling are given in Money (n. 3).

13. One Oregonian mushroom develops under water and sheds its spores into the river. The Buller's drop mechanism would be disrupted by contact with water, but this fungus traps air between its gills, allowing the usual mechanism to operate. The spores accumulate beneath the gills in wedge-shaped piles that separate from the bottom of the cap and drift downstream. This beautiful mushroom was described by J. L. Frank, R. A. Coffan, and D. Southworth, *Mycologia* 102, 93–107 (2010).

14. W. Elbert et al., *Atmospheric Chemistry and Physics* 7, 4569–4588 (2007). The total atmospheric emission of spores from all kinds of fungi was estimated at 50 megatons per year. The diversity of fungi contributing to air particulates is addressed by J. Fröhlich-Nowoisky et al., *PNAS* 106, 12814–12819 (2009).

15. R. Jaenicke, *Science* 308, 73 (2005).

Chapter 3

1. The name *grisette* is applied to various species of *Amanita* with gray or brown caps, including *Amanita vaginata* and *Amanita fulva* (the tawny grisette), and

so my friend was wrong in identifying *Amanita muscaria* as a grisette. The term refers to a cheap gray dress fabric worn by working girls in France, and to the girls themselves.

2. T. N. Sherrat, D. M. Wilkinson, and R. S. Bain, *The American Naturalist* 166, 767–775 (2005). Only one-tenth of the European species included in this survey were poisonous. The authors defined "poisonous" as "a range of effects ranging from relatively mild illness to death," which reads like the warnings of side effects on most prescription medicines.

3. This idea was suggested to me by Michael Kuo, author of a number of excellent mushroom books and editor of the marvelous website www.mushroomexpert.com

4. G. C. Ainsworth, *Introduction to the History of Mycology* (Cambridge: Cambridge University Press, 1976).

5. Saccardo's monumental 160,000-page, 26-volume work, *Sylloge Fungorum Omnium Hucusque Cognitorum*, or, "summary of all fungi known up to this time" (Patavii: 1882–1972) dealt with thousands of microfungi in addition to mushrooms.

6. P. Sunnerhagen and J. Piškur, eds., *Comparative Genomics: Using Fungi as Models*, Topics in Current Genetics vol. 15 (Berlin, Heidelberg, New York: Springer, 2006).

7. F. Martin et al., *Nature* 452, 88–92 (2008). This was followed by the sequencing of the genome of the ink cap (or inky cap), *Coprinopsis cinerea*: J. E. Stajich et al., *PNAS* 107, 11889–11894 (2010).

8. S. L. Miller et al., *Mycologia* 98, 960–970 (2006) addresses *Russula*'s relationships; Jefferson's paternity case was illuminated by E. A. Foster et al., *Nature* 396, 27–28 (1998) and E. A. Foster et al., *Nature* 397, 32 (1999).

9. R. P. Korf, *Mycotaxon* 93, 407–415 (2005).

10. E. O. Wilson initiated an online project, launched in 2008, called the *Encyclopedia of Life* (www.eol.org), that is inspired by the task of documenting all of the living species known to science and adding new ones as they are discovered. Wilson discussed the concept earlier in *TRENDS in Ecology and Evolution* 18, 77–80 (2003). The relationship between this project and the protection of biological diversity is discussed by S. N. Stuart et al., *Science* 328, 177 (2010). The Jim Morrison quote comes from his poem, "American Night," performed on the album by The Doors titled "An American Prayer" (Elektra/Asylum Records, 1978).

11. J. W. Taylor and C. E. Ellison, *PNAS* 107, 11655–11656 (2010).

12. J. N. Robinson, *Geology* 15, 607–610 (1990).

13. W. M. R. F. Schwarze, J. Engels, and C. Mattheck, *Fungal Strategies of Wood Decay in Trees*, translated by W. Linnard (Berlin, New York: Springer, 2000); F. H. Tainter and F. A. Baker, *Principles of Forest Pathology* (New York: John Wiley, 1996).

14. R. A. Blanchette, *Mycologia* 89, 233–240 (1997), and *Mycologist* 15, 4–9 (2001).

15. P. Bodensteiner et al., *Molecular Phylogenetics and Evolution* 33, 501–515 (2004).

16. Y. Terashima and A. Fujiie, *International Turfgrass Society Research Journal* 10, 251–257 (2005).

17. J.-H. Choi et al., *ChemBioChem* 11, 1373–1377 (2010).

18. Dew from inside fairy rings was believed to spoil the complexion. F. M. Dugan, *North American Fungi* 3, 23–72 (2008).

19. V. Rudolf, *American Folklore* 66, 333–339 (1953).

20. J. Ryall, *National Geographic News* (April 19, 2010).

21. To guess at the number of hyphae in a fairy ring with a radius of 5 meters, I assumed that the most active part of the mycelium formed a torus with radius of 10 centimeters. This torus would be planted in a volume 2 million cubic centimeters of soil. With an estimated 10,000–1 million hyphae growing in every cubic centimeter, this equates to a total of 20 billion–2 trillion hyphae in a single ring. Gareth Griffith, professor at University of Wales Aberystwyth, was kind enough to check this estimate. His book chapter on grassland fungi provides an excellent discussion of fairy rings: G. W. Griffith and K. Roderick, in *Ecology of Saprotrophic Basidiomycetes*, edited by L. Boddy, J. C. Frankland, and P. van West (London: Academic Press, 2008), 277–299.

22. U. G. Mueller et al., *Quarterly Review of Biology* 76, 169–197 (2001); M. W. Moffett, *Adventures among Ants: A Global Safari with a Cast of Trillions* (Berkeley: University of California Press, 2010).

23. J. P. E. C. Darlington, in *Nourishment and Evolution in Insect Societies*, edited by J. H. Hunt and C. A. Nalepa (Boulder, Col.: Westview Press, 1994), 105–130.

24. J. Korb, *Naturwissenschaften* 90, 212–219 (2003).

25. This is probably the world's largest fruit body, though even bigger ones are reported from time to time from South America, though these reports are never supported by a photograph with a scale. *Macrocybe titans* is another giant, with fruit bodies almost as large as those of *Termitomyces titanicus*. This species grows in Mexico and in Central and South America. It has been studied in Costa Rica, where it colonizes abandoned nests of leaf-cutter ants.

26. There is some uncertainty about the original author of the term "symbiosis". Albert Frank used it in an 1877 paper on lichen anatomy, and the great mycologist Anton de Bary published a monograph on the subject in 1879.

27. S. E. Smith and D. J. Read, *Mycorrhizal Symbiosis*, 3rd edition (New York: Academic Press, 2008).

28. Martin et al. (n. 7).

29. The *Laccaria* genome, consisting of 20,000 genes, is much larger than the 6,000-gene genome of baker's yeast, *Saccharomyces cerevisiae*, and the 10,000 genes of the filamentous ascomycete fungus, *Neurospora crassa*.

30. D. Martinez et al., *Nature Biotechnology* 22, 695–700 (2004).

31. J. N. Klironomos and M. M. Hart, *Nature* 410, 651–652 (2001).

32. Eighty percent of all plants form mycorrhizal associations with fungi. The most common of these are arbuscular mycorrhizae, produced by fewer than 200 species of fungi within the Phylum Glomeromycota. Nutrient transfer between fungus and host occurs through intricately branched microscopic structures called arbuscules that are formed by the fungus inside the living root cells of their plant hosts. Other kinds of mycorrhizae are called ectendomycorrhizae, and arbutoid, monotropoid, ericoid, and orchid mycorrhizae.

33. Smith and Read (n. 27).

34. It is possible that fungi continue to supply nutrients to green orchids in adulthood, particularly when the plants are growing in shady habitats.

Chapter 4

1. After a ten-month convalescence, Pennypacker's bravery was rewarded with promotion to the rank of Brigadier General. He was only twenty years old. Galusha Pennypacker (1844–1916) is the youngest officer to have held the rank of general in the United States Army.

2. C. McIlvaine, *One Thousand American Fungi: How to Select and Cook the Edible; How to Distinguish and Avoid the Poisonous* (Indianapolis: Bowen-Merrill, 1900).

3. Charles McIlvaine to Curtis G. Lloyd, October 2, 1898. C. G. Lloyd, Mycological Correspondence, Lloyd Library and Museum, Cincinnati, Ohio. McIlvaine refers to spending the winter in his "city residence," in Colebrook, Pennsylvania (close to Mt. Gretna), to complete his forthcoming book, *Five Hundred Toadstools and How to Cook Them.*

4. Besides his mycological writings, McIlvaine published magazine articles and poetry, a novel titled *A Legend of Polecat Hollow: An American Story* (London: Ward, Lock & Co., 1884), and a collection of essays for children, *Outdoors, Indoors, and Up the Chimney* (Philadelphia: The Sunday School Times Company, 1906). He published *Polecat Hollow*, and much of his other work, under the pseudonym Tobe Hodge. In *Polecat Hollow* and other pieces, he sought to capture the dialect of Appalachia. Here are a couple of snippets: "I wuz borned in that cabin tar. The old un wuz burned down jist afore my time, but I mind fayther goen, when he were an ole man, a diggin fer to see ef he could find any sign uv the two children thet wuz burned in it" (p. 9); "Way back yander, long 'nough afore the white people came to Elk; there was nothen but Ingin this hull kintry" (p. 19).

5. J. A. Palmer, *The Popular Science Monthly* 11, 93–100 (1877).

6. J. A. Palmer, *Mushrooms of America: Edible and Poisonous* (Boston: L. Prang & Co., 1885).

7. D. W. Rose, *McIlvainea* 16, 37–42, 52–55 (2006). This article by David Rose is filled with fascinating details on the roots of amateur mycology in the United States.

8. R. Watling, *Fungi* (London: The Natural History Museum, 2003), p. 86.

9. S. Egli et al., *Biological Conservation* 129, 271–276 (2006).

10. J. A. Jackson (editor), *Bird Conservation 3* (Madison: University of Wisconsin Press, 1988), p. viii.

11. W. E. Schlosser and K. A. Blatner, *Journal of Forestry* 93, 31–36 (1995).

12. S. A. Alexander, J. F. Weigand, and K. A. Blatner, *Environmental Management* 30, 129–141 (2002).

13. *The Japan Times Online*, October 26, 2007.

14. The matsutake that grows in Asian pine forests is a different species, called *Tricholoma matsutake*. The Japanese harvest in 1950 was 6,484 tons (metric tons), and only 65 tons in 2006 (n. 13). Insect damage to forests and climate change, rather than overpicking, are thought to have been responsible for this dramatic decline. Matsutake imports from the United States increased from 51 tons in 1993 to 284 tons in 1997. Source: E. Boa, *Wild Edible Fungi: A Global Overview of Their Use and Importance to People* (Rome: Food and Agriculture Organization of the United Nations, 2004). Over the same time period, imports of the Asian species from China were quite steady, averaging 1,122 tons per year.

15. I have spoken about mushroom conservation, developing the kind of argument that I'm making in this chapter, on a couple of National Public Radio programs, and I wrote an essay, "Why Picking Wild Mushrooms May Be Bad Behavior," that was rejected by a number of journals before its publication in *Mycological Research* 109, 131–135 (2005). I received some angry e-mails from mushroom enthusiasts who could not conceive that their activities might have negative effects upon their quarry, along with a similar number expressing support. All of the angry messages came from Americans; most of the supportive ones from Europeans. I think that this may have something to do with the enduring fantasy of the endless frontier for many of my fellow American citizens.

16. D. Arora, *Mushrooms Demystified*, 2nd edition (Berkeley, Calif.: Ten Speed Press, 1986).

17. D. Arora and G. H. Shepard, *Economic Botany* 62, 207–212 (2008).

18. R. L. McLain, *Economic Botany* 62, 343–355 (2008). This article has a spectacularly Kafkaesque title: "Constructing a Wild Mushroom Panopticon: The Extension of Nation-State Control over the Forest Understory in Oregon, USA."

19. W. S. Sun and J. Y. Xu, *Edible Fungi of China* 18, 5–6 (1999). Assuming, for the purpose of this highly fanciful calculation, that the average mushroom weighs 25 g, the Chinese pick 12 billion fruit bodies every year in China, which is equivalent to nine mushrooms per person. This is a bit less than commercial mushroom production in the United States, which is estimated at 370,000 tons; source: www.americanmushroom.org

20. D. Arora, *Economic Botany* 62, 278–290 (2008).

21. Boa (n. 14).
22. E. T. Yeh, *China Quarterly* 161, 264–278 (2000).
23. McLain (n. 18).
24. Most of the stinkhorns sold in China are cultivated.
25. Excellent books on the edible ascomycetes include M. Kuo, *Morels* (Ann Arbor: University of Michigan Press, 2005), and I. R. Hall, G. T. Brown, and A. Zambonelli, *Taming the Truffle: The History, Lore, and Science of the Ultimate Mushroom* (Portland, Ore.: Timber Press, 2007).
26. J. Cherfas, *Science* 254, 1458 (1991).
27. M. M. Gyosheva et al., *Mycologia Balcanica* 3, 81–87 (2006).
28. A. Dahlberg and H. Croneborg (compilers), *33 Threatened Fungi in Europe* (Swedish Environmental Protection Agency and European Council for Conservation of Fungi, 2003).
29. http://www.iucn.org
30. J. Gerard, *The Herball, or, Generall Histories of Plantes* (London: Iohn Norton, 1597).
31. T. Baker, *Mycologist* 4, 25–29 (1990). Early English names for mushrooms and toadstools included: tadstooles, mousheroms, muscheron, toodys hatte, toad's cap, toad's meat, toad's cheese, musserouns, tadstoles, frogge stoles, frogstooles, frog stool, frog's cheese, paddocstol, paddokstole, paddockstool, puddockstool, toad's paddock, padockchese, Tommy toad, toad's kep, frog sates, and moushrimpes. John Ramsbottom provides a lively discussion of the etymology in his *Mushrooms and Toadstools: A Study of the Activities of Fungi* (London: Collins, 1953).
32. A. Ubrizsy Savoia, *Physis* 20, 49–69 (1978).
33. M. Dash, *Tulipomania: The Story of the World's Most Coveted Flower and the Extraordinary Passions It Aroused* (New York: Crown, 1999).
34. F. van Sterbeeck, *Theatrum Fungorum* (Antwerp: Joseph Jacobs, 1675).
35. An essay that I wrote on Sterbeeck's illustrations (N. P. Money, *Inoculum* 58(5), 1–2 [2007]), stimulated an interesting critique by an Australian mycologist, Heino Lepp (H. Lepp, *Inoculum* 59(1), 12–13 [2008]). Lepp argued that when Sterbeeck used the Flemish phrase *naer het leven* to refer to the origin of his illustrations, he might have meant "true to life," rather than the alternative translation of "from life." The late Geoffrey Ainsworth, from whom I took my cue, had pursued the "from life" interpretation in his marvelous scholarly book, *Introduction to the History of Mycology* (Cambridge: Cambridge University Press, 1976). According to the "true to life" translation, however, Sterbeeck might have meant that his illustrations were accurate depictions of the mushrooms without implying that the illustrations were based upon direct observations made during his forays. Indeed, in some cases, Sterbeeck says that his illustrations come from Clusius, which argues against any intentional deception. Thus far, Lepp offers a logical defense of

Sterbeeck. The Hungarian scholar who examined the *Codex* in 1900, Gyula Istvánfii, however, pointed to specific examples in which Sterbeeck misrepresented *Codex* illustrations as his own. (Istvánfii published high-quality reproductions of the watercolors in an elephant-sized book titled *Etudes et Commentaraires sur le Code de l'Éscluse* [Budapest: G. Istvánfii, 1900].) Lepp suggests that, rather than pointing to minor differences between mushrooms in the *Codex* and mushrooms in Sterbeeck's work and concluding plagiarism, we should not be surprised by similarities among the images of the same species in *Theatrum Fungorum* and the *Clusius Codex*. Perhaps my tribulations in dealing with instances of plagiarism in the university classroom have made me overly sensitive to the issue, but those similarities look more like copies to me. In conclusion, regarding this mote of mycological history, I'm not sufficiently impressed by the case of Sterbeeck's innocence to ruin a good story whose interest is heightened, as I said in my 2007 essay, by the whiff of deceit from the Renaissance.

36. A. Ubrizsy Savoia, in F. Egmond, P. Hoftijzer, R. Visser, *Carous Clusius: Towards a Cultural History of a Renaissance Naturalist* (Amsterdam: Royal Netherlands Academy of Arts and Science, 2007), pp. 267–292.

37. D. Pegler and D. Freed, *The Paper Museum of Cassiano dal Pozzo, Series B—Natural History, Part 2, Fungi*, 3 volumes (London: Royal Collection Enterprises, 2005).

38. R. E. Machol and R. Singer, *McIlvainea* 1(2), 14–18 (1973).

39. D. P. Rogers, *Mycologia* 69, 223–245 (1977); C. L. Shear and N. E. Stevens, *Mycologia* 11, 181–201 (1919).

40. J. Webster, *Mycological Research* 10, 1153–1178 (1997).

41. The article from the *Daily News* was reprinted in *Transactions of the Woolhope Naturalists' Field Club* 1874–5–6, 135–136 (1880).

42. R. D. Bixler, *Results: National Survey of Mushroom Club Members* (2008). Ninety percent of the 1,141 respondents to this survey (57% women) said that they cook with mushrooms. Niche mushroom-related activities included dyeing cloth with mushrooms (4%), and making paper with mushrooms (2%). The survey also revealed that members of American mushroom clubs spent an average of $750 in 2007 on mushroom books and collecting equipment, travel related to mushrooming, club memberships, and so on. This represents a national economic stimulus of $855,750.

Chapter 5

1. The comparison is based on a robotic picking rate of thirty mushrooms per minute versus eighteen per minute for humans who pick for eight hours per day for one week. In published trials, robots picked at only half the speed of humans,

but, according to engineers, "future commercial robots could easily exceed manual picking rates." Source: J. N. Reed et al., *Journal of Agricultural Engineering Research* 78, 15–23 (2001).

2. W. Hanbury, *A Complete Body of Planting and Gardening: Containing the Natural History, Culture, and Management* …. (London: E. and C. Dilly, 1770–1771). The French botanist Joseph Pitton de Tournefort (1656–1708) wrote an earlier description of the Parisian method of mushroom cultivation: *Mémoires de l'Académie des Sciences de Paris* 58–66 (1707). Tournefort surmised that the white threads (hyphae and bundles of hyphae) in manure develop from mushroom seeds (spores).

3. D. Badham, *A Treatise on the Esculent Fungeses of England* … (London: Reeve, 1847).

4. B. M. Duggar, *Mushroom Growing* (New York: Orange Judd Company, 1915).

5. W. Robinson, *Mushroom Culture: Its Extension and Improvement* (London: Frederick Warne and Co., 1870).

6. Robinson (n. 5).

7. M. Harland, *Common Sense in the Household: A Manual of Practical Housewifery* (New York: C. Scribner & Co., 1872).

8. S.-T. Chang and P. G. Miles, *Mushrooms: Cultivation, Nutritional Value, Medicinal Effect, and Environmental Impact*, 2nd edition (Boca Raton, Fla.: CRC Press, 2004). Annual data on mushroom cultivation are compiled by the National Agricultural Statistics Service (NASS), Agricultural Statistics Board, U.S. Department of Agriculture (http://www.americanmushroom.org/nass.htm)

9. B. E. Mowday, *Chester County Mushroom Farming* (Charleston, SC: Arcadia, 2008).

10. *Agaricus bisporus* has a single gene that controls mating type or sex. This comes in two versions, or alleles. In preparation for spore formation, two nuclei of opposite mating type fuse inside the basidium, and this diploid nucleus undergoes meiosis to produce four nuclei: two of each mating type. Self-fertility is maintained by an intricate mechanism ensuring that both of the spores receive one nucleus of each mating type. If a spore receives two nuclei of the same mating type, it cannot form a colony capable of producing mushrooms on its own, nor is it competent to mate. The life cycle of *Agaricus bisporus* is an example of "secondary homothallism."

11. N. P. Money, *The Triumph of the Fungi: A Rotten History* (New York: Oxford University Press, 2007). The phenomenon of "inbreeding depression," or reduced fitness due to inbreeding, has been studied in *Agaricus bisporus* by J. Xu, *Genetics* 141, 137–145 (1995).

12. A. M. Kligman, *Handbook of Mushroom Culture* (Lancaster, Pa.: Business Press, 1950), p. 138.

13. A. S. M. Sonnenberg, in *Science and Cultivation of Edible Fungi*, edited by L. J. L. D. Van Griensven (Rotterdam: Balkema, 2000), p. 2539.

14. P. Stamets, *Growing Gourmet and Medicinal Mushrooms*, 3rd edition (Berkeley, Calif.: Ten Speed Press, 2000).

15. R. W. Kerrigan, *Canadian Journal of Botany* 73, S973–S979 (1995).

16. See Chang and Miles (n. 8), and Stamets (n. 14) for more information on mushroom cultivation.

17. Chang and Miles (n. 8).

18. J. J. P. Baars et al., in *Science and Cultivation of Edible Fungi*, edited by L. J. L. D. Van Griensven (Rotterdam: Balkema, 2000), pp. 317–323.

19. M. Kuo, *Morels* (Ann Arbor: University of Michigan Press, 2005).

20. E. Danell and F. J. Camacho, *Nature* 385, 303 (1997).

21. I. R. Hall, W. Yun, and A. Amicucci, *TRENDS in Biotechnology* 21, 433–438 (2003).

22. Hall, Yun, and Amicucci (n. 21).

23. P. Stamets, *Mycelium Running: How Mushrooms Can Help Save the World* (Berkeley, Calif.: Ten Speed Press, 2005).

24. Stamets (n. 14).

25. P. Kalač, *Food Chemistry* 113, 9–16 (2009).

26. G. Rückert and J. F. Diehl, *Zeitschrift für Lebensmittel-Untersuchung und- Forschung* 185, 91–97 (1987).

27. Kalač (n. 25). Mushroom fiber is not the same as plant fiber. The insoluble fiber in lettuce is in the form of microfibrils of cellulose that constitute the bulk of the walls that surround every cell. Fungi don't produce cellulose; instead, they wrap their cells with skeins of chitin microfibrils that constitute much of the fiber content of a mushroom.

Chapter 6

1. *Tricholoma equestre* is also known as *Tricholoma flavovirens*. The Latin name *Russula subnigricans* has also been applied to a North American species, *Russula eccentrica*; it is not clear whether this is a separate species from the toxic mushroom that is found in China and Japan.

2. K. H. McKnight and V. B. McKnight, *Peterson Field Guide: A Field Guide to Mushrooms: North America* (New York: Houghton Mifflin Harcourt; Rei Sub edition, 1998); J.-L. Lamaison and J.-M. Polese, *The Great Encyclopedia of Mushrooms* (Königswinter: Könemann, 2005); T. Læssøe, A. Del Conte, and G. Lincoff, *The Mushroom Book: How to Identify, Gather, and Cook Wild Mushrooms and Other Fungi* (New York: DK Publishing, 1996); B. Dupré, translated by D. Macrae, *World Treasury of Mushrooms in Color* (New York: Galahad Books, 1974); R. Courtecuisse and B. Duhem, *Collins Field Guide: Mushrooms and Toadstools of Britain and Europe* (London: Harper Collins Publishers, 1995).

3. Lamaison and Polese (n. 2).

4. R. Bedry et al., *The New England Journal of Medicine* 345, 798–802 (2001).

5. M. Matsuura et al., *Nature Chemical Biology* 5, 465–467 (2009).

6. This compound was isolated from fruit bodies collected in Kyoto (western Japan), where all of the poisonings have occurred. Fruit bodies from northeast Japan containing different toxic compounds called *russuphelins* may belong to a different species.

7. P. Nieminen, M. Kirsi, and A.-M. Mustonen, *Experimental Biology and Medicine* 231, 221–228 (2006).

8. P. Nieminen, M. Kirsi, and A.-M. Mustonen, *Food and Chemical Toxicity* 47, 70–74 (2009).

9. The range in dosage depends upon the method used to calculate equivalent body mass; mice have a much larger surface-area-to-volume ratio than apes have, and this scaling factor should be considered in relating mouse to human toxicity data.

10. A. Levin, *The Mail on Sunday* (September 5, 2010).

11. J. Fyall, *The Scotsman* (November 8, 2009).

12. A. I. K. Short et al., *Lancet* 316: 942–944 (1980). Mistaking the mushrooms for chanterelles, two men and one woman made a stew from *Cortinarius speciosissimus*; both men required kidney transplants; the woman recovered renal function after a few days. There is some evidence that women may be less susceptible to kidney damage caused by webcaps.

13. http://news.bbc.co.uk/2/hi/uk_news/7752103.stm

14. M. Kuo, http://www.mushroomexpert.com/russula.html (July 2011).

15. Fyall (n. 11).

16. H. Frank et al., *Clinical Nephrology* 71, 557–562 (2009).

17. D. R. Benjamin, *Mushrooms: Poisons and Panaceas—A Handbook for Naturalists, Mycologists, and Physicians* (New York: W. H. Freeman and Company, 1995). This is a marvelous book for those interested in learning more about mushroom poisoning.

18. Benjamin (n. 17).

19. F. M. Dugan, *Fungi in the Ancient World: How Mushrooms, Mildews, Molds, and Yeast Shaped the Early Civilizations of Europe, the Mediterranean, and the Near East* (St. Paul, Minn.: APS Press, 2008).

20. Benjamin (n. 17).

21. A. Pringle et al., *Molecular Ecology* 18, 817–83 (2009).

22. A.-M. Dumont et al. *Lancet* 317, 722 (1981); J. M. Bauchet, *Bulletin of the British Mycological Society* 17, 110–111 (1983).

23. A. Coombs, *Nature Medicine* 15, 225 (2009).

24. D. Michelot and L. M. Melendez-Howell, *Mycological Research* 107, 131–146 (2003).

25. Annual statistics on poisoning are compiled by the American Association of Poison Control Centers and are available on its website: www.aapcc.org

26. J. Jaenike et al., *Science* 221, 165–167 (1983); J. Jaenike, *Evolution* 39, 1295–1301 (1985). Recent studies question the conclusions of this earlier work on toxin tolerance among flies, and there is a lot of scope for further experiments.

27. S. Camazine, *Journal of Chemical Ecology* 9, 1473–1481 (1983). According to R. G. Wasson (whose work is discussed in Chapter 7), reindeer may also be attracted to fly agarics. If true, this observation would be further testament to the failure of hallucinogens to discourage predation.

28. T. N. Sherratt, D. M. Wilkinson, and R. S. Bain, *The American Naturalist* 166, 767–775 (2005); T. Lincoln, *Nature* 437, 1248 (2005).

29. F. M. Dugan, *North American Fungi* 3, 23–72 (2008).

30. B. H. Shadduck, *The Toadstool Among the Tombs* (B. H. Shadduck, 1925).

31. The importance of recognizing the toxic minority of fruit bodies while collecting mushrooms was exploited hideously by the Nazi writer Ernst Hiemer in his illustrated collection of stories for children, *Der Giftpilz* (or *The Poisonous Mushroom*) (Nuremberg: Stürmerverlag, 1938). The cover illustration shows a caricature of Jews as green-hued death caps, and the stories describe the heroism of children who recognize the insidious threat that they pose to "the fatherland." The book's publisher, Julius Streicher, was executed for war crimes in 1946.

32. E. Dickinson, *The Complete Poems of Emily Dickinson* (Boston: Little, Brown, and Company, 1924), Part 2, Nature, XXV.

33. Dugan (n. 29).

34. For literary revelry in mushroom power, see R. Roehl and K. Chadwick (eds.), *Decomposition: An Anthology of Fungi-Inspired Poems* (Sandpoint, Idaho: Lost Horse Press, 2010).

35. S. Plath, *The Collected Poems* (London: Faber and Faber, 1981), 139–140. Plath wrote "Mushrooms" in 1959.

36. B. Kingsolver, *Prodigal Summer* (New York: HarperCollins, 2000).

37. W. P. K. Findlay, *Fungi: Folklore, Fiction, & Fact* (Richmond, UK: The Richmond Publishing Company, 1982).

38. D. E. Desjardin, A. G. Oliveira, and C. V. Stevani, *Photochemical and Photobiological Sciences* 7, 170–182 (2008); D. E. Desjardin, et al., *Mycologia* 102, 459–477 (2010). Bioluminescence seems to have evolved multiple times among the mushrooms, producing light-emitting species of *Omphalotus*, *Armillaria*, *Mycena* (and related genera), and species in a fourth lineage of fungi that has yet to be named. Both the mushrooms and the mycelia of some species glow, while, in others, only the fruit body or the supporting colony luminesce.

Chapter 7

1. M. P. English, *Mordecai Cubitt Cooke: Victorian Naturalist, Mycologist, Teacher and Eccentric* (Bristol, U.K.: Biopress, Ltd., 1987).

2. M. C. Cooke, *The Seven Sisters of Sleep: Popular History of the Seven Prevailing Narcotics of the World* (London: James Blackwood, 1860).

3. A. Letcher, *Shroom: A Cultural History of the Magic Mushroom* (London: Faber and Faber, 2006).

4. J. F. W. Johnston, *The Chemistry of Common Life*, 2 volumes (Edinburgh: W. Blackwood, 1854–1855). *Amanita muscaria* is treated in the second volume.

5. D. Michelot and L. M. Melendez-Howell, *Mycological Research* 107, 131–146 (2003). Muscimol binds to the $GABA_A$ receptor altering neuronal activity in the cerebral cortex, hippocampus, and cerebellum.

6. P. J. von Strahlenberg, *An Historico-Geographical Description of the North and Eastern Parts of Europe and Asia* (London: W. Innys and R. Manby, 1736).

7. J. U. Lloyd, *Etidorhpa* (Cincinnati: J. U. Lloyd, 1895). The work of John's brother, Curtis Gates Lloyd (1859–1926), is discussed in N. P. Money, *Mr. Bloomfield's Orchard: The Mysterious World of Mushrooms, Molds, and Mycologists* (New York: Oxford University Press, 2002).

8. The hollow-earth theory had been very popular in the Cincinnati area earlier in the nineteenth century, when John Cleeves Symmes Jr., a local veteran of the Revolutionary War, declared in a pamphlet that, "the earth is hollow, habitable within," and went on to petition Congress for funding for an expedition to the North Pole to find an entrance. There were predictable jokes about "Symmes' Hole" among his contemporaries—"How far is the earth from Symmes' Hole? Same distance as Uranus," would be my opening adolescent quip—but Symmes was part of a tradition of hollow earthers, including the astronomer Halley, and the theory was accepted quite widely.

9. M. Carmichael, in *Psychedelia Britannica: Hallucinogenic Drugs in Britain*, edited by A. Melechi (London: Turnaround, 1997), pp. 5–20.

10. English (n. 1).

11. M. C. Cooke, *The Seven Sisters of Sleep: The Celebrated Drug Classic* (Rochester, Vt.: Park Street Press, 1997).

12. M. C. Cooke, *Edible and Poisonous Fungi: What to Eat and What to Avoid* (London: Society for Promoting Christian Knowledge, 1894).

13. R. G. Wasson, G. Cowan, F. Cowan, and W. Rhodes, *Maria Sabina and Her Mazatec Mushroom Velada* (New York: Harcourt Brace Jovanovich, 1974), text accompanied by musical score, prepared by W. Rhodes, and four cassette tapes. The Mushroom Velada, or night vigil, arranged for a sick teenage boy, was held in 1958. María began by telling the boy that he would get well and then, after consultation with the mushrooms, informed him in a very forthright manner of his impending death. According to Wasson, María's prophecy came true: the boy died a few weeks after the ceremony. Additional recordings of chanting by María Sabina at an earlier mushroom ceremony in 1956 are archived on the Smithsonian Institution's Folkways Recordings website and can be downloaded from www.folkways.si.edu

14. Wasson, Cowan, Cowan, and Rhodes (n. 13), p. 107.
15. P. Stamets, *Psilocybin Mushrooms of the World: An Identification Guide* (Berkeley, Calif.: Ten Speed Press, 1996).
16. M. Wittmann et al., *Journal of Psychopharmacology* 21, 50–64 (2007). Psilocin binds to the 5-HT$_{2A}$ receptor and, with lower affinity, to 5-HT$_{1A}$.
17. Stamets (n. 15).
18. R. R. Griffiths et al., *Psychopharmacology* 187, 268–283 (2006). Subjects were given psilocybin or methylphenidate (Ritalin) in each session and neither subjects nor their monitors knew which substance they had been given. Ritalin is prescribed for the treatment of attention deficit hyperactivity disorder (ADHD) and was chosen for the study because it affects patients as swiftly as psilocybin, lasts for the same length of time, and also produces mood-altering effects.
19. Wittmann (n. 16).
20. R. R. Griffiths et al., *Journal of Psychopharmacology* 22, 621–632 (2008).
21. LSD is produced from lysergic acid; lysergic acid is produced from ergotamine, a natural compound produced by the ergot fungus, *Claviceps purpurea*, or from a related compound called ergine produced by plants. The ergots are hardened resting structures called sclerotia that the fungus forms on its plant hosts. The ergots also contain lysergic acid.
22. Griffiths et al. (n. 20).
23. N. Tuno, H. K. Takahashi, H. Yamashita, N. Osawa, and C. Tanaka, *Journal of Chemical Ecology* 33, 311–317 (2007).
24. J. Ramsbottom, *Mushrooms and Toadstools: A Study of the Activities of Fungi* (London: Collins, 1953).
25. Michelot and Melendez-Howell (n. 5).
26. J. M. Allegro, *The Sacred Mushroom and the Cross: A Study of the Nature and Origins of Christianity within the Fertility Cults of the Ancient Near East* (London: Hodder and Stoughton, 1970).
27. M.-L. Espiard et al., *European Psychiatry* 20, 458–460 (2005). This paper described recurrent flashbacks (perceptual disturbances) in an eighteen-year-old man eight months after he had eaten magic mushrooms and smoked cannabis.
28. H. de Wit, *Psychopharmacology* 187, 267 (2006).
29. de Wit (n. 28).

Chapter 8

1. M. Adams, NaturalNews.com (Oct. 23, 2009). This website is a reliable source of unfounded, illogical, and potentially harmful advice for the unwary. In one of his mushroom postings Adams wrote about "a blend of 17 extremely powerful medicinal mushrooms, almost all of which have known anti-cancer benefits." According to this online sage, "It's a well-known scientific fact that

Medicinal mushrooms have the ability to prevent, treat and even *reverse* cancer, and that's why everywhere in the world other than the United States, they're called 'anti-cancer mushrooms.' Furthermore, this product is "so effective at boosting the immune system and preventing cancer that the FDA actually went after the [company that markets this] and made them censor their description to remove any hint of what this product can actually do" (NaturalNews.com, Jan. 21, 2009). Ah, the truth is out, it's the federal government again, meddling in our God-given American affairs, making sure that honest folks with "terminal" cancer aren't informed about the miracle cure available in the form of capsules filled with powdered mushrooms.

2. www.botanicalpreservationcorps.com, accessed May 12, 2010.

3. Quotes from www.fungus.com, accessed May 12, 2010. The same quotes appear in Fungi Perfecti's printed catalog.

4. P. Stamets, *Growing Gourmet and Medicinal Mushrooms*, 3rd edition (Berkeley, Calif.: Ten Speed Press, 2000).

5. http://www.cordycepsreishiextracts.com/polyporus_umbellatus_medical_research_references.htm

6. Mushrooms escaped stronger regulation with the passage of the Dietary Supplement Health and Education Act of 1994.

7. From Fungi Perfecti's printed catalog Fall 2009–Summer 2010.

8. The Dietary Supplement Safety Act of 2010 was an effort to grant the FDA additional authority over dietary supplements. Support for this bill wavered in 2011 and its fate is unclear at the time of writing.

9. Many studies have affirmed consumer support for increasing government regulation of dietary supplements, including R. J. Blendon et al., *Archives of Internal Medicine* 161, 805–810 (2001). On a nonmycological note, I was very pleased by the FTC's recent order to Kellogg's to desist from claiming that its breakfast cereals "support your child's immunity" (*New York Times*, June 12, 2010). One can guess at the banality of the discussions at marketing meetings of breakfast cereal companies that strategized the recasting of ambiguous information on antioxidants into a guilt trip for parents in grocery stores.

10. B. M. Ley, *Discover the Beta Glucan Secret! For Immune Enhancement Cancer Prevention & Treatment Cholesterol Reduction Glucose Regulation & Much More!* (Detroit Lakes, Minn.: BL Publications, 2001). Dr. Ley writes that, "She is dedicated to God and to spreading the health message."

11. J. E. Smith, N. J. Rowan, R. Sullivan, *Medical Mushrooms: Their Therapeutic Properties and Current Medical Usage with Special Emphasis on Cancer Treatments* (London: Cancer Research UK, 2002).

12. A. T. Borchers et al. *Experimental Biology and Medicine* 233, 259–276 (2008).

13. www.mdanderson.org/education-and-research/resources-for-professionals/clinical-tools-and-resources

14. *Ganoderma tsugae* looks almost identical to *Ganoderma lucidum*, but it grows on conifers. The relationships among different species of *Ganoderma* are unclear, and some of them can be difficult to separate using morphological features or genetic analysis.

15. Stamets, n. 4.

16. C. Hobbs, *Medicinal Mushrooms: An Exploration of Tradition, Healing, and Culture* (Summertown, Tenn.: Botanica Press, 1986).

17. T. Aoki et al. *The Lancet* 936–937 (Oct. 20, 1984). There are some related conference proceedings from the 1980s on hemophiliac patients, but nothing that merited publication in a peer-reviewed journal.

18. www.anti-aids.net

19. T. Muta, *Current Pharmaceutical Design* 12, 4155–4161 (2006).

20. H. Hall, *Skeptic Magazine* 15, 4–5 (2010).

21. A. Weil, *The Natural Mind: An Investigation of Drugs and the Higher Consciousness* (Boston: Houghton Mifflin, 1972).

22. A. S. Relman, *The New Republic* (Dec. 14, 1998).

23. Weil told the story of his miraculous cure during an interview in 2001 with Ed Bradley for the CBS News program *60 Minutes* and has repeated the story in many other venues. The story of the cure is depersonalized in his book *Health and Healing* (Boston: Houghton Mifflin, 1983), p. 241: "I once watched a man with a lifelong cat allergy play with a cat several hours after taking a dose of LSD. ... "

24. G. Guzman, F. Tapia, P. Stamets, *Mycotaxon* 65, 191–195 (1997). In a more recent act of mycological homage, an African species of phallic mushroom, the diminutive stinkhorn *Phallus drewesii*, was named for Robert Drewes, a curator at the California Academy of Sciences. The good-natured Drewes said, "It's a wonderful honor and great fun to have this phallus-shaped fungus named after me. I have been immortalized in the scientific record." He was quoted in *ScienceDaily.com* (June 15, 2009). The taxonomic description was authored by D. Desjardin and B. Perry, *Mycologia* 101, 545–547 (2009).

25. www.drweil.com; www.origins.com

26. There is another reason why one might be wary about using mushrooms in cosmetics. Mushrooms can cause allergic skin reactions, including contact dermatitis. These are seen in people who work with mushrooms, including mushroom pickers and sorters, but any facial products that contain mushrooms cannot claim to be hypoallergenic.

27. L. J. L. D. Van Griensven, *International Journal of Medicinal Mushrooms* 11, 281–286 (2009).

28. Chilly, because evaporative cooling of this large mushroom drops its internal temperature by as much as 5°C, and its clammy cap feels cold to the touch. J. Husher et al., *Mycologia* 91, 351–352 (1999).

INDEX

Accademia dei Lincei, 93
Adams, Mike, 158, 192–193n1
Agaricus bisporus. See button
   mushroom
Agaricus campestris. See meadow
   mushroom
Agaricus silvicola, 21
Agaricus xanthodermus. See yellow
   stainer
AIDS, 168–169
Albatrellus ovinus, 119
Aleurodiscus amorphous, 7
Allegro, John, 154
Amanita bisporigera. See
   destroying angel
Amanita caesarea. See Caesar's
   mushroom
Amanita muscaria. See fly agaric
Amanita phalloides. See death cap
amateur mycology, 82, 124
Amanitopsis nivalis, 80
antioxidants, 172–174
Armillaria ostoyae, 8, 62
Armillaria tabescens, 31
Arora, David, 87–88

artist's fungus (*Ganoderma
   applanatum*), 40–42, 62, 166
ascomycetes, 39–40
Auricularia auricula. See wood ear
Auriscalpium vulgare, plate 4

basidia, 18
Bastien, Pierre, 128–129
Battarra, G. A., 116
beefsteak fungus (*Fistulina
   hepatica*), 61–62, plate 7
Berkeley, Miles, 94
Beta-glucans, 163–164
bioluminescence, 136, 139,
   190n38
birch polypore (*Piptoporus
   betulinus*), 42, 61
bird's-nest orchid (*Neottia
   nidus-avis*), 76
blood-foot mushroom (*Mycena
   haematopus*), 2, plate 1
boletes, 57, 75–76, 79–80, 85,
   88–89, 131
Boletus, 75, 79–80
Boletus edulis. See porcini